PRINTED
TEXTILE
DESIGN

LAURENCE KING

Published in 2013 by
Laurence King Publishing Ltd
361-373 City Road
London EC1V 1LR
Tel: +44 20 7841 6900
Fax: +44 20 7841 6910
e-mail: enquiries@laurenceking.com
www.laurenceking.com

This book was designed and
produced by Laurence King
Publishing Ltd, London.

A catalogue record for this book is
available from the British Library.

ISBN: 978 1 78067 118 5

Design: Eleanor Ridsdale
Editor: Debra Johnston Cobb

Cover: 'Bamboo Birds' designed by
Lucy Wilhelm. © Friulprint SRL

Contents page: 'Hollis' by
Surfacephilia

Printed in China

LAURENCE KING PUBLISHING

PRINTED TEXTILE DESIGN

AMANDA BRIGGS-GOODE

CONTENTS:

INTRODUCTION

Printed textile design is a creative field of practice and a dynamic and exciting industry that encompasses fashion, interior fabrics and wallpaper, cards and stationery, as well as textile art and craft. Printed textile designers develop the images, patterns and colours that are intrinsic to the aesthetics, application and successful sales of these printed products.

Printed textile designers work as part of a large industry. The designs they create may be used by fashion brands or in products for soft furnishings and interior design for retail sale to consumers. They may also be used in 'contract' products or corporate clothing for hotels, hospitals or other companies. Because printed textiles are ubiquitous, the contribution of the print designer can often be overlooked while the product application becomes the focus. You are probably more likely to know the names of several fashion designers than the identity of a textile designer – they are generally anonymous. Printed textile designers can work independently, in design studios or directly for retailers or manufacturers.

Printed Textile Design is about the skills, knowledge, techniques and processes needed to pursue a career in printed textile design. With case studies from practising designers, inspirational examples from the industry as well as practical activities, the book reveals approaches and strategies to support your development in becoming a printed textile designer.

Printed textile designers work within a context that requires them to be able to initiate and interpret design inspiration, taking into consideration consumer trends, fashion forecasts and design requirements of different market levels, and to do so through an understanding of the heritage and history of the design styles and printing processes of this field. By placing printed textile design in this broad context, this book recognizes its inherent value and its contribution to design and culture.

Developing experience in the fundamental design skills of drawing, colour and repeat will enable you to begin the process of exploring and developing your design inspiration with a clear sense of direction. The design development process that you pursue may take you through digital design and/or the print room to explore a range of visual effects; this book describes a range of such processes to support this part of your journey.

The book also explains the commercial aspects of the market, as well as examining ethical parameters in terms of your design choices of fabrics, print processes and dyes. Understanding the impact of these materials and processes, the decision-making process and the supply chain for different markets, products and price-points is essential to give you a broader understanding of how the industry operates.

Through case studies, the book demystifies the design process and shows how creative and skilled designers are able to develop new and exciting work while responding to the commercial demands of the industry. Finally, the book describes various opportunities for working within the industry, along with methods that will enable you to prepare your portfolio and make approaches to the industry for internships or jobs.

Printed Textile Design offers an holistic perspective on the role of the printed textile designer. The book also functions as an essential guide to enable you to become fully aware of the context, design fundamentals and industrial parameters of the printed textile design industry.

Opposite: Rachel Trenouth, 'Captured Apparition Design 3'. Textile printing can be described as the application of colour to fabric using defined marks, shapes and patterns.

1
DESIGN IN CONTEXT

INTRODUCTION
DESIGN IN CONTEXT

In this chapter we will define the context within which printed textile designers develop and resolve design collections for manufacture in the fashion or interior markets. When printed textile designers are considering how to respond to a design brief (an outline of the project's design parameters) they will begin by synthesizing and considering their knowledge and experience of four main strands, or components that provide context for the project: design inspiration; design styles and print heritage; market levels; and trend prediction. The interpretation of these strands will form the backdrop or foundation for the designer's creative work.

Design inspiration will be specific to the brief the designer is working with, and might include a concept, theme, colour palette and product application. The first step may be creating a mood board to assist the designer in maintaining a focus for ideas. The mood board may include the designer's own or found imagery to suggest ideas for colour, image, texture, style or product application.

Printed textile designs tend to be organized into style categories, of which the four main ones are floral, geometric, conversational and world cultures. Each of these categories has sub-sections; understanding their characteristics enables you to communicate and respond to a design brief by articulating a breadth of design ideas, both visually and verbally. The heritage of historical printing processes influences and shapes printed textile design, not only through the varied techniques used to transfer images onto cloth, but also through its visual library of image qualities, from which you can choose for image-making purposes, according to the style you wish to develop. While some of these processes are now redundant or exist only in small niche markets, the styles that are associated with them have their own qualities of line, effects or layouts.

Textile designers must also be aware of the framework in which the industry operates, which includes market levels and trend cycles. Market levels, which can be described as being high, mid or mass, define the price-point of a product and the type of consumer who may purchase it. The market level influences the decisions that designers make in relation to the development of their design collection. We might find that the same types of image may be simplified or made more challenging, depending on whether the market level is low or high. A higher price-point may mean that the product uses more luxury fabric or more complex processes than would a product with a lower price-point, where mass production requires standardization and cheaper raw materials.

Textile design and manufacturing function within the 'fashion system', which enables the industry to control the process of 'planned obsolescence' by creating demand for new products while enabling retailers to minimize risk. This is done for both interiors and fashion through international trend prediction and fashion forecasting companies. Trend changes are processed and communicated through colour cards, publications, the Internet and at trade fairs. These tools are intended to guide the design or development of products for a particular season in terms of mood, colour, image and materials.

Previous pages: Sophie Bard, 'Watery Fabric'. Understanding the characteristics of various print styles provides the print designer with a set of design ideas with which to begin a creative project.

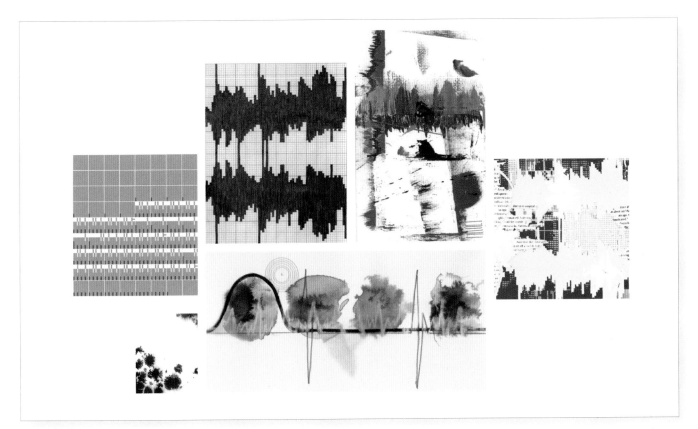

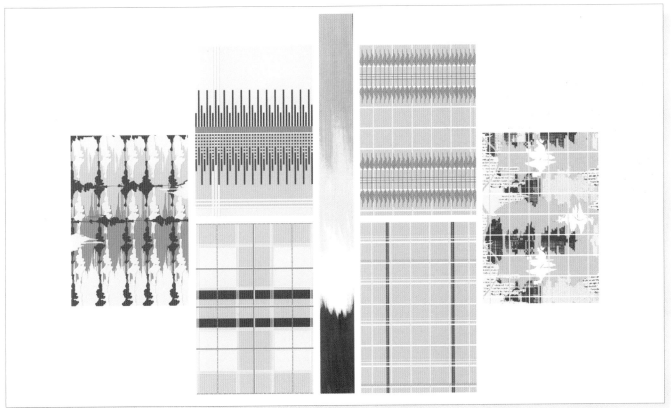

Top: This mood board by Anna Piper shows her design inspiration in terms of colours, marks, scale and proportion.

Above: In Anna Piper's final design collection we can see how her designs incorporate the linear qualities and 'accidental' marks seen in her mood board.

THE DESIGN BRIEF

A design brief is assigned by a client or developed by the designer, and functions as an outline of the project's design parameters. These generally include: the concept, theme or inspiration, perhaps with some visual examples; the target market or consumer; the product application (fashion, interiors, womenswear or menswear, etc.); and the colour palette, which may refer to a colour trend or a particular range of colours chosen by the client.

The design brief should also outline the client's expectations: the number of designs (a collection usually contains between six and ten); any technical requirements; size and colour limitations; and whether design repeats are needed. In some businesses the brief may also include information about how the design will be manufactured, the type of fabric to be used, and the time-scale and costing required. A brief may be just a paragraph or it can be more expansive.

This brief should provide enough information for you to begin the process of researching and developing ideas for your design inspiration – the theme for your drawings, photographs or imagery that you will employ to develop your collection successfully and fulfil the brief. The heritage of printed textiles helps support design thinking at this stage, in that previous design styles and printing processes can influence the way in which you move forward with your theme. You also need to consider the trend predictions and market level appropriate to your project.

An example of a commercial design brief entitled 'Vintage Feminine' reads as follows:

> For a mass-market womenswear collection you should explore pattern and colour to develop dramatic and memorable prints, using soft base tones mixed with intense colours such as powder blue, aqua, primrose and hot pink to suggest a vintage inspiration. Abstract imagery can be offset with vintage florals, and layered with images of lace and embroidery to further suggest the concept of feminine beauty through elegant draping. Drama can be added with a playful and contrasting approach to scale and proportion.

> The collection should include a minimum of eight designs, in repeat, for use at the mass-market level. Colourways will utilize the given palette in combinations of up to eight colours; alternative colourways are optional. The prints should be appropriate for screen printing on feminine, floaty fabrics for women's dresses and separates, and the project should include visualizations using your designs. Your print designs will be the focal point of the project, and must demonstrate a creative yet commercial approach.

In another example, design student Sophie Bard uses her primary design inspiration to create a design brief for her own collection called 'Lost in a Parisian Wilderness'. In the process she provides an excellent picture of the research, inspiration and connective steps used in developing a design collection:

Paris is the main inspiration because of the beautiful design aesthetics of the city, and the concept is inspired by a day spent wandering around Paris.

The variety of visual inspiration I found in Paris will allow me to work towards an eclectic aesthetic and to produce drawings of different elements: animals, birds and butterflies; musical instruments; jewellery; vintage fashion figures; sky, clouds and light; flowers; architecture; ornate gold details; and clocks and timepieces. References to Art Deco and Art Nouveau are notable in these elements, and I am trying to convey a luxurious decadent feeling in my designs to link to the moods of the periods.

I am inspired not only by Art Deco and Art Nouveau artists such as William Rowe, but also by Surrealism and the dreamlike illustrations of contemporary designers such as Pomme Chan, Vault 49 and Uberpup. The collection also includes ideas for a lighting concept, inspired by the work of design collectives such as Assume Vivid Astro Focus, wallpaper designer Maria Yaschuk and Patternity Studio, who integrate lighting with exciting surface imagery.

From these starting points, I will be creating a collection of designs for interiors that will include a group of installation pieces comprising decorative lighting panels. The panels will be covered in digitally printed surface designs with an illustrative/conversational aesthetic contrasting their simplistic silhouettes, with laser-cut shapes through the panels that allow the lighting behind to shine through.

The project will be more innovative than trend-led, aiming at the high-end markets. The wall art and range of prints would be suitable for use in cutting-edge spaces such as hotels and nightclubs, or in smaller, exclusive business spaces such as a boutique or concept store.

I would like to work with a sophisticated group of colours, experimenting with metallics (with reference to Parisian architecture) and heavy use of black, white and greys, with emphasis on pencil drawings.

This collection of images from Sophie Bard shows a range of visual research and design ideas created and developed as she evolved her design collection. These photographs, linear sketches and detailed drawings all enabled her to explore various concepts, colour palettes and styles. Time taken to develop and synthesize design ideas is crucial in the crystallization of a design inspiration to be employed in the resolution of the brief.

As you can see, Sophie has written her brief with an already established inspiration, based on her initial research in Paris and supported by researching artists and art movements relevant to the development of her imagery. She has also started to give her work a context and a product application by assessing the marketplace and designers producing similar work.

DESIGN INSPIRATION

The first step towards answering a design brief begins with researching your design inspiration. With your design brief in mind, the search for design inspiration should include the exploration of a wide range of ideas and influences. Brainstorming and creating mind maps tend to be good ways of developing keywords and ideas and can also help you begin to group them. From this you may collect and research as broadly as possible themes and images that might connect and inspire your thinking.

Designers will often describe how they search for new ideas constantly when they are visiting new places – recording observations in sketches, photographs or notes. Architecture, travel or other cultural experiences provide visual imagery that might support this research. Other places that could provide visual inspiration for a particular brief may include collections or special exhibitions in museums, galleries or archives, vintage or craft fairs, or cultural festivals. It might also be useful to think more broadly about popular culture forms, such as film, advertising or music, that conjure a particular mood or vibe that fits the brief.

When beginning visual research you should record some of these ideas in a sketchbook – drawing, creating and/or photographing objects, shapes, textures and colours through which you can start to investigate your theme. Drawing with a variety of tools or media, or drawing directly onto a computer, or manipulating or collaging images and textures can help to develop these themes further.

When you have established the visual inspiration you will use in the resolution of your design brief, you may begin to bring this research together in a mood board, or by pinning the inspiration to a wall as a constant visual reminder of the brief to help keep you focused. Designers are often avid collectors of images, photographs, fabric, books and postcards and buttons, etc., and may keep them for years before finding the right time to use them as a significant inspiration for a design collection. The way in which you organize these images – the layout, colour combinations and linking images – can also help you make new connections and solutions.

Mary Crisp, a printed textile designer working in the automobile industry, describes her design inspiration as being eclectic:

It can be in everything I see, from the rain dripping down the window to the new piece of graffiti near my house. I see different things, try to make a mental note and I then try to imitate them through my design work, which is usually constructed digitally whenever I sit down at a computer.

I still think it is so important to have a wide spectrum of art influences, from architecture to ceramics, jewellery and digital media. There are magazines that are a good way to see these influences, and exhibitions are fantastic for new inspiration.

Gilly Thorne is a print designer for interior fabrics based in Australia. She spends a lot of time travelling to the USA and Europe to gather research and visit trade fairs:

These trips are primarily aimed at trend shopping – in all of the major department stores and, of course, in the smaller independent shops, boutiques and fabric stores for both fashion and interiors . . . We then return . . . and do a trip report and colour and design presentation. We create colour palettes for the season (we work a year ahead) and print trend and ideas booklets for the designers and other design managers in the studio.

Ideas for your collection can also develop from more unlikely sources. Anna Scott, a print designer for menswear, describes how she builds her design inspiration:

We look at what people are wearing on the street. This extends to out-of-work-time, too – if I am out in town I look at what men are wearing. I just went to a music festival and took lots of sneaky pictures. Celebrities are important, too. All this research is tailored to what fits with our customer and what we will sell.

On trips abroad, ideas might be generated from looking at what the factories can achieve; perhaps someone is using a great print technique and that will give you an idea.

All of the designers stress the importance of doing 'primary' research through observing and recording, then trying to develop the visual qualities they have identified into their own work, either directly or through abstracting the imagery. The goal is to develop these ideas in their own unique way, but with relevance to the commercial context in which they work.

Sometimes what inspires you is not something you can collect or study, but something more ethereal: a mood or a concept. While it may be more challenging to capture or create images or effects that work in this way, such design inspirations can create novel and exciting work.

Opposite: A mind map, like this one by Nahim Akhtar, can be helpful for you to develop keywords and establish ideas by linking thoughts. This should assist you in shaping your project and give you a sense of direction for your design journey.

IDEAS BRAINSTORM

TRANSLATING TRADITIONAL WEAVE TO INSPIRE PRINT DESIGN...

PRODUCT

Initial research – exploring florals: trips to gardens, Tropical World, etc., to gain inspiration from drawings and get a feeling of the traditional William Morris colour palette and the textural grounds found in the surfaces

Using research samples and designers to inform product ideas – looking at fragmented structures and the amalgamation of traditional coloured flowers alongside linear drawings – drawing with different scales and mixed media

Producing textile scarf samples for the commercial fashion retail market

Progression of 'tapestry' and 'hand-woven' prints through time

CONCEPT

Begin by exploring the history behind tapestry weaving and how designs have developed through time

Traditional tapestry prints – exploring the relationship and contrast between William Morris-style motifs and more contemporary, linear patterns

Possible processes to take further from initial drawings – screen printing, devoré and discharge to explore the textural qualities?

Digital printing?

First-hand research – using the available jacquard software to help inform my design concept

Audience – need to research into the anticipated consumer and recent catwalk shows, etc., to inform my prints

MARKET

Exploring the originality and beauty of traditional printing techniques and effects (woodblock) – something lost within some harsh, overstated, imitative fashion

Experimenting with broken structures (fragmented lines) as an exploratory stage prior to developing my designs in CAD

MATERIALS

Creating a varied range of scales/colour swatches to work from and experiment with

Development – photograph samples on mannequins to envisage the flow of fabrics over the body prior to progressing into CAD for my final designs and making the collection more coherent

- 100% silks
- Fine or woven?
- Texture?
- Neutral or busy grounds?

Laser-cutting?

Fabric research needs to be carried out well in advance to my exploratory stage to aid my understanding of the product I intend to print

RESEARCH DEVELOPMENT

Colour palette – explore trends

Research into the high street/upmarket-level fashion trends: high-end department stores, galleries, museums, etc.

Research cultures/ colour schemes and different print scales and how they represent various notions

Kaleidoscopic art?
* Karin Bergman *

Exploring artists that incorporate placement florals in their work, the traditional (fabrics for interiors) of William Morris and others

DESIGN STYLE AND PRINT HERITAGE

In developing your own personal approach to the design brief you may also consider if there are design styles or aspects of print processes with visual effects that might support your design inspirations further. These might include qualities of image, texture, line, organization or layout that you can incorporate into your visual research and design development.

Design styles in printed textiles have developed over centuries and have emerged into clearly established categories that relate to the types of imagery that are found within this area of textile design. The four main groups are floral, geometric, world cultures and conversational.

In general, the name of each category speaks for itself: florals will feature flowers and/or other plant life, geometrics will refer to imagery that utilizes non-organic imagery or is abstract (stylized without the source of the original material being apparent); world cultural styles can be linked to a specific location or anthropological group; and conversationals can be described as imagery that references popular icons of a particular time period or season, or which is unique and challenges our perceptions in some way.

These categories make reference to a range of criteria, such as the type of imagery, how the image has been developed, the geographic location the style emerged from, the visual effects the style creates, how colour has been used, and relationships to wider design and art movements.

There are many other terms that define print styles, and this wider vocabulary enables a more detailed visual understanding of each category. These style terms include: florals – chintz, Indiennes, ditsy, organic; geometrics – trompe-l'œil, stripes, allover, spots or polka dots, tartan, architectural, paisley, checks, gingham; world culture – folkloric, Chinoiserie, oriental; conversational – animal prints, psychedelic, camouflage. There are also terms that could apply to any style, such as abstract or photographic. These four main categories are often intermixed; you might have floral imagery interspersed with a geometric design, for example.

While these are not hard-edged categories, they are established ways of referencing the visual qualities you may be researching or developing. It is important for designers to be able to recognize, understand and interpret each style where relevant to their brief or design ideas.

The various historical and contemporary printing processes also have a visual heritage that the print designer can use as a design tool. These processes define the way in which patterns are translated onto cloth, as each technology involved in printing creates unique visual effects of image, texture and colour. While some printing methods are now redundant as commercial processes, they continue to have a stylistic influence in contemporary printed textile design. These effects can be interpreted by designers when creating their own image-making style.

Textile printing methods can be categorized in the following ways: resist printing, where an image is printed or painted using a resist before dyeing; relief printing processes, such as woodblock; gravure or intaglio, such as copper plate or roller printing; stencilling, for example, screen printing; transfer printing, often completed using a heat source; and, most recently, digital printing, which utilizes an inkjet process.

Inspired by the art of the Dutch Masters (in this case Jan Davidsz de Heem's Bouquet in a Glass Vase*), Wendy Braithwaite's still lifes explore their detailed style, capturing surface qualities against a typically dark background, which further illuminates the colours within the objects.*

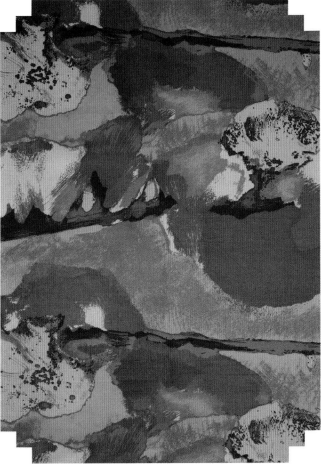

FLORAL

Top left: This floral design, produced at the Wiener Werkstätte in 1913 by Josef Hoffmann, is abstract and two-dimensional.

Top right: Designed by William Morris in 1873 and block printed by Thomas Wardle, this Arts & Crafts floral is typical of their work in both motif and layout.

Bottom left: 'Wild Bloom' is a large-scale design created by Doreen Dyall for Hull Traders in the 1960s that uses expressive and textural marks to produce this four-colour print on cotton satin.

FLORAL

Left: Josef Frank, designing in the 1920s, is renowned for his use of simplicity and strong colour to create fresh and naïve designs, such as 'Milles Fleur' here.

Right: The 'Floribunda' pattern, here on Tana Lawn, was designed in the early 1980s for Liberty Art Fabrics by Allan Thomas. It uses sprigs and singular flowers in a style often described as 'ditsy'.

GEOMETRIC

Left: The impact of 1960s Op Art is strongly evident in this design by Barbara Brown, which was produced for Heal's fabrics in 1967.

Right: This dynamic 1923 geometric by Liubov Popova is a powerful example of the design aesthetics that emerged during the Russian Revolution of the 1920s.

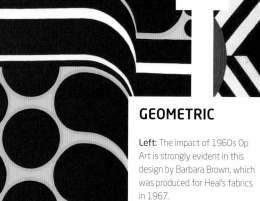

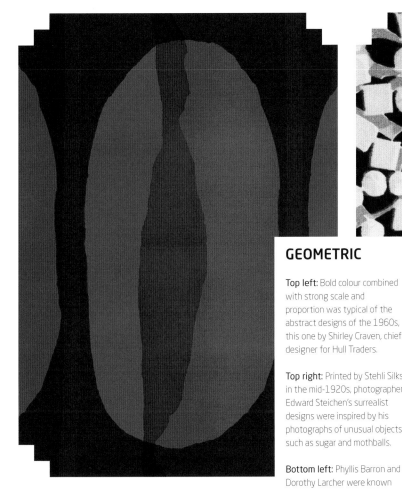

GEOMETRIC

Top left: Bold colour combined with strong scale and proportion was typical of the abstract designs of the 1960s, this one by Shirley Craven, chief designer for Hull Traders.

Top right: Printed by Stehli Silks in the mid-1920s, photographer Edward Steichen's surrealist designs were inspired by his photographs of unusual objects such as sugar and mothballs.

Bottom left: Phyllis Barron and Dorothy Larcher were known for their woodblock and lino handprints, which reflected the eclectic English modernism of the 1920s and '30s.

Bottom right: This design from the 1950s, 'Fibra' by Esther Haraszty, uses a limited colour palette and line quality with spontaneous spatial organization of the line-and-hole formation to create a complex design.

CONVERSATIONAL

Top left: Alec Walker's abstract designs on silk for Crysede are characterized by their painterly, spontaneous quality and vibrant colour palette.

Top right: Created in the 1970s by Jane Sandy for Heal's, 'Nimbus' combines Op Art with the Photorealism that was becoming fashionable at the time.

Bottom left: Trompe l'œil effects were a big interior trend in the 1980s as demonstrated in this design called 'Panache' by Anne White.

Bottom right: Emily Charman has created a textile collection that uses an illustrative style to interpret English cultural identity in a humorous and quirky way.

Opposite page, top: Eddie Squires's confident, dramatic designs for Warners in the 1960s and '70s utilized current events, such as the moon landing, and photographic techniques that challenged contemporary commercial printing.

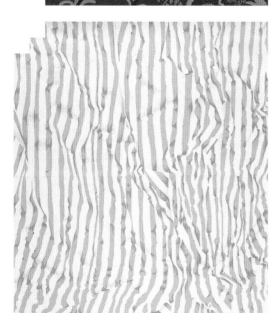

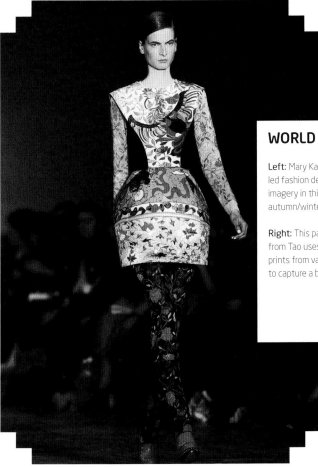

WORLD

Left: Mary Katrantzou, a textile-led fashion designer, uses oriental imagery in this collection for autumn/winter 2011/2012.

Right: This patchworked pattern from Tao uses ikat and Indienne prints from various world cultures to capture a bohemian style.

RESIST PRINTING

An early form of printing, the resist style utilizes a substance to resist, or block, the dyestuff from the fabric, such as clay or rice paste, with the most common contemporary example being wax. An image or pattern is applied in wax by hand with a brush or a tool known as a *tjanting*, or via a more mechanized version, which is a *tjap* or block version. When the wax or other resist has been added to the fabric, the cloth is then cold-water dyed and the patterned, or resisted, area is protected from the dye. After boiling the fabric to fix the dye and remove the wax, the pattern remains as the base colour of the original fabric.

This technique is associated in particular with Javanese fabrics since 960 AD. The process of drawing with hot wax demands that the designs are created quickly, and this leads to linear designs that are rhythmic and allow the designers and the wax to flow smoothly. Commonly, these textiles are repeatedly waxed and then dyed to enable the designer to build more complex designs. The colours used in the dyeing process are typically blue, brown and black.

This exquisite batik work of around 1930 from Java is an example of resist printing. Note the white line around all of the individual elements of the design, painted using a *tjanting* tool and hot wax.

WOODBLOCK PRINTING

While block printing is generally associated with woodblocks, there are examples of blocks being made from terracotta or metal, initially for paper printing, in China some 2,000 years ago. India was also significant in developing block printing and continues to produce exquisite and highly valued examples.

The process involves a skilled craftsman carving a pattern or image into wood and this 'relief' image is then pressed into dye. Using pressure and a type of hammer known as a maul, the ink is transferred to the fabric. The size of the blocks varies, but as they are lifted and pressed by one person they need to be manageable in size and weight.

This process can produce simple one-colour prints or be more complex and use several blocks, with each introducing a different image and colour to the textile. If the design is going to repeat across the fabric, pins inserted into the block can be used to line up, or 'register', the design. This printing method began as industrial manufacture in Europe from the mid-seventeenth century and became the main process for printing textiles by the nineteenth century.

The type of visual effects that we see in block printing tend to be flat and to sit on one plane with stylized qualities. There is not a great deal of texture in the imagery.

William Morris, an important designer in the nineteenth century and one of the main drivers of the Arts and Crafts movement, used this process for the production of wallpapers and textiles for his various companies. The process of block printing, which was a highly skilled job, fitted strongly with the Arts and Crafts philosophy, which promoted the idea that 'crafts' and 'skills' ensured a more fulfilling work experience. Morris collaborated with dyer and chemist Thomas Wardle, who was inspired by the sophisticated natural dyestuffs and patterns of Indian block printing. Their iconic block-printed patterns are considered a benchmark in English textiles and continue to be inspirational and commercially popular to this day.

Joyce Clissold, a textile designer who studied in the 1920s, became the chief designer for Footprints, a block-printing workshop that had great success and continued producing textiles until the 1980s. Clissold worked with block printing as part of the creative process, often using lino instead of wood because it was easier to cut and use.

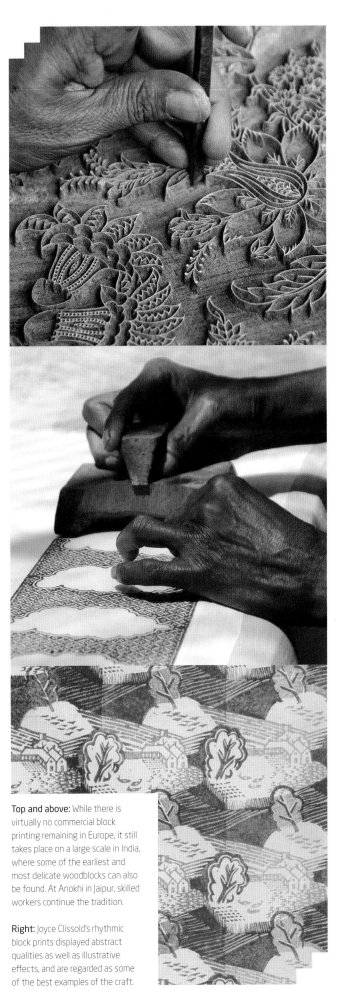

Top and above: While there is virtually no commercial block printing remaining in Europe, it still takes place on a large scale in India, where some of the earliest and most delicate woodblocks can also be found. At Anokhi in Jaipur, skilled workers continue the tradition.

Right: Joyce Clissold's rhythmic block prints displayed abstract qualities as well as illustrative effects, and are regarded as some of the best examples of the craft.

COPPER PLATE PRINTING
(GRAVURE OR INTAGLIO)

Copper plate printing is a method that first appeared in Europe in the mid-eighteenth century. This process involves images being incised or engraved onto a metal plate (usually copper) and is known as an intaglio method. Dye is applied to the surface of the plate; the excess is then scraped away, leaving the remainder only within the incised lines. This dye is then transferred to cloth by applying pressure.

This process allowed the use of much finer linear marks and cross-hatching in printed designs and enabled more varied tonal qualities than had previously been possible. The types of image associated with this process were romanticized rural or mythological scenes and were typically printed in one colour: red, blue or purple.

Another characteristic of this printing process was the use of layout and organization. The copper plates were often very large and this presented difficulties in repeating the imagery; as a result, 'island designs' emerged, whereby the imagery sits alone within its own space, disconnected from the other elements. The best designs ensure that the space between the islands is managed in a way that provides a visual cohesion.

The distinct visual language of this process is often replicated today in contemporary textile design, either directly utilizing similar romanticized scenes or ironically subverting them by using more contemporary or challenging images.

Above and left: The copper plate prints that emerged from the print works of Jouy, France, from 1759 were praised for their fine line and tonal effects, and came to be known as toiles de Jouy. Here, a traditional design on fabric and a flat plate are accompanied by tools used for incising the metal.

Left : Timorous Beasties' 'Toile Collection' uses the same island-image organization, single colour and linear elements as toiles de Jouy, but with a twist: contemporary urban imagery replaces the traditional scenes of rural life.

Right: Vivienne Westwood was inspired by toiles de Jouy in these designs from 1996, contrasting the simplicity of the garments with the scale and complexity of the imagery.

Far right: Fashion designer Jeremy Scott playfully combines toile de Jouy references with an eighteenth-century silhouette and styling.

ENGRAVED ROLLER PRINTING

As the Industrial Revolution took hold and interest in mechanization grew, the engraved metal plate was transformed into a metal roller, with the aim of increasing the speed of printing and production. By 1785, new mechanical approaches enabled methods for engraving designs onto the metal roller, which allowed for more variations of line, texture and tone. The level of detail that was possible with these engraved methods was superior to other print processes of the time; and the engraved metal roller was capable of printing both the finer detail of the copper plate as well as the broad effects of block printing.

Above: Advances in mechanization led to the engraved copper roller, which enabled a wider range of printing possibilities in terms of scale, repetition, continuity of image and number of colours.

Left: A copper roller print from the 1830s, showing the quality of line and detail that could be achieved with this process.

SCREEN PRINTING

Metal roller printing opened the way for the photo-engraving of screens and rotary screen printing, both of which were developed in the early twentieth century. These enabled printed patterns to move beyond linear or solid colour imagery, making shaded effects a more practical possibility.

Screen printing works on the principle of stencilling – a very ancient print process that has been used to create sophisticated and intricate designs, particularly in Japan, since the eighth century. To produce a paper stencil, the areas intended for print are removed by cutting or tearing. Paper stencils are often used today for quick creative prints with spontaneous qualities.

Screen printing uses a woven mesh stencil, originally silk. A tool known as a squeegee, which is usually a rubber blade, is used to push ink or dye through the stencilled pattern onto the fabric. First introduced to Europe from Asia in the late eighteenth century, this method was popularized in England for printing wallpaper fabrics early in the twentieth century.

Screen-printed images produce spontaneous, fluid and painterly print styles that can be used creatively and innovatively in contemporary design. During the 1910s the photo-imaging of stencils was introduced, and when popularized in the 1920s this technique offered a more fluid interpretation of a designer's style than had been previously achievable within an industrial context.

Just as copper plate printing transformed into roller printing, screen printing was adapted to the form of a rotating cylinder in the 1960s, creating a low-cost process for mass manufacturing. Tubular screens filled with print paste rotate at the same velocity as the fabric; the paste is forced into the fabric as it is pressed between the plate and a continuous rubber printing blanket. This method is currently the fastest and most economical printing process for a large meterage of fabric.

Screen printing's limitations include the need for colour separations, as each colour in a pattern must have its own screen, which adds expense. Most screen prints use no more than five or six colours; this limit challenges the designer to use fewer colours to greater effect.

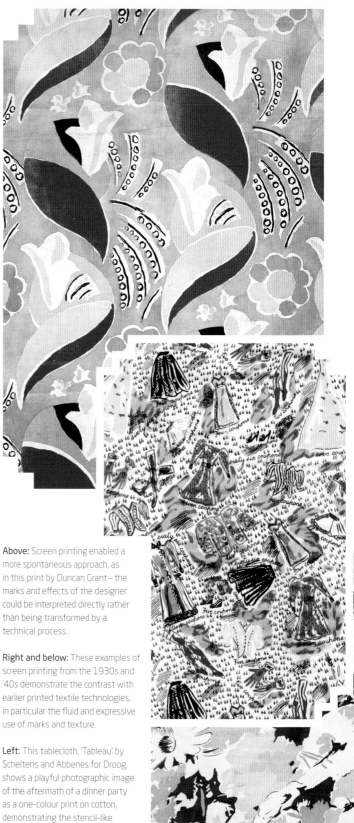

Above: Screen printing enabled a more spontaneous approach, as in this print by Duncan Grant – the marks and effects of the designer could be interpreted directly rather than being transformed by a technical process.

Right and below: These examples of screen printing from the 1930s and '40s demonstrate the contrast with earlier printed textile technologies, in particular the fluid and expressive use of marks and texture.

Left: This tablecloth, 'Tableau' by Scheltens and Abbenes for Droog, shows a playful photographic image of the aftermath of a dinner party as a one-colour print on cotton, demonstrating the stencil-like qualities of screen printing.

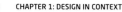

HEAT TRANSFER PRINTING

The commercial development of transfer printing occurred during the 1960s. It involves the printing or painting of transfer inks onto paper that then adhere to certain fabrics under specified heat-controlled conditions.

There are several methods of industrial heat transfer but the most commercially viable is 'sublimation' printing. The sublimation process turns the dye printed on the paper, which is a solid, into a gas, and then returns it to a solid again as it is transferred to the fabric. The paper can be printed using any method, including digital, and this has increased the scope and the range of imagery available to this process.

While this method was significant in opening up the printing of photographic imagery onto textiles, it is limited in that it can only be used with synthetic fabrics, primarily polyester. With the development of many new and innovative synthetic performance fabrics for active sportswear, heat transfer printing has found a solid niche in the market.

Transfer inks can be also be painted straight onto paper and then transferred using an iron or a heat press directly onto fabric, allowing designers to take a more spontaneous approach in the studio.

The heritage of heat transfer printing emerged from a new range of images, including those with photographic qualities, which could be printed onto fabrics using more colours than could be achieved with other print methods. The process also increased the number of tones that were achievable, and this led to what became known as illusionary prints. These designs created the illusion of a heavyweight woven textile printed on a finer and lighter fabric.

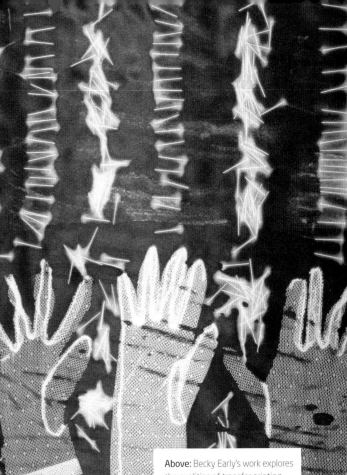

Above: Becky Early's work explores the qualities of transfer printing using found objects and a 'collaging' technique that leaves a ghostly memory of the object.

Below: In this unique collaboration between the fashion designer Hussain Chalayan and clothes label Puma, the densely decorated image is transferred to polyester fabric; the complex design is controlled partly through a limited colour palette.

DIRECT INKJET (DIGITAL) TEXTILE PRINTING

Digital printing is a relatively new printing process. An inkjet printhead places micro-droplets of dye onto the fabric in a pattern controlled by a computer-aided design, or CAD, program, eliminating the need to engrave separate screens for each colour. Over the past 20 years digital printing has evolved from a mechanism used to speed up the sampling process to an exclusive tool used at the upper end of the market, where its high costs can be absorbed. As the technology continues to develop, higher speeds and improved inks and pigments have brought about lower costs and wider distribution, enabling mass production rather than only exclusive small runs.

From a design perspective, digital printing and CAD have dramatically altered the types of image that can be explored and created within printed textiles. The ability to print full-colour, multi-layered and detailed designs using unlimited changes in scale or repeat, non-repeating elements, or prints engineered to product shapes, has provided designers with creative challenges and led to the emergence of new, exciting and vibrant printed textiles.

Digital printing can capture and reproduce a large range of image qualities, and is capable of using millions of colours to translate the subtleties and nuances of the original images on to fabric. The number of colours that are economically viable in a rotary screen print may no longer be a concern if a shift occurs towards digital inkjet printing in the global mass market.

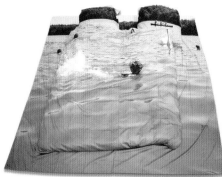

Repeat and image continuity are also vitally important to textile production and design. When using non-digital printing methods the repeat of the fabric needs to be established to enable print production to occur in an efficient and practical way, and there are defined sizes of repeating pattern. However, with CAD-driven digital printing the repeat can occur over much larger areas, and non-repeating patterns also can be commercially viable. The ability to use repeat and pattern in this way may enhance a garment or interior product through the creative use of variation in design.

Digital printing also enables the design and production of engineered prints that are developed in unison with specific garment shapes. This offers textile designers the opportunity to consider more challenging uses of imagery in relation to the end use, the shape of the body or interior products.

Evidence of the impact of digital printing and its applications can be found at trade fairs, where textile designers and fabric companies are selling their work. You can now see textile designs being sampled on fabric, rather than paper, and the sense of scale and proportion can be visualized on a two- or three-dimensional garment shape.

Top: Basso & Brooke exploit the potential that digital development brings to the resolution of their ideas. Here seaming is used to interrupt imagery and juxtapose floral and textural images.

Above: Digital printing allows the designers of this 'Lake' bedding for Bless to use challenging photographic imagery that interacts with three-dimensional form.

Right: Mary Katrantzou uses digital printing to explore the relationship between imagery, garment and three-dimensional shape with intelligence and creativity.

UNDERSTANDING THE PRINTED TEXTILE MARKET

It is important to recognize that retailers and brands operate within distinct market levels, creating differentiation and catering to consumer preferences. It is critical to understand the market level of your customer as designated by the design brief, as this will influence how you develop your designs (including your motifs, layout and use of colour) and how you utilize resources such as fabric, print processes and special effects. In general terms, retail markets tend to be split into three distinct levels: high, mid and mass.

The highest level tends to be designer-led, which carries with it the requirements of exclusivity, quality, luxury and high price level. Designer products set rather than follow trends, and as such will use innovative imagery to make a strong style statement. They are expected to use the highest-quality fabrics and to be constructed using the best manufacturing techniques.

Printed embellishment and brand identity add to the value of a product. While the cost of a printed process used at the designer level may be high, the middle and mass markets may eventually introduce the process as well, impacting upon the perception of exclusivity. For example, the recent trend for foiling, initiated at the high end of the market, was copied at all levels of the market, mainly on T-shirts; as a result, the top end has moved away from this process.

Both Paul Smith and Timorous Beasties produce products at the high end of the market, which is characterized by the quality of cloth, exclusivity, print and manufacturing techniques.

Paul Smith, a uniquely British fashion designer, pays great attention to production details, using contrast fabric inside cuffs and collars or engineered imagery, worked so that the design moves around the body smoothly. Paul Smith's printed garments always demonstrate a strong relationship between the form and the print; considering how the design flows where the shirt meets across the buttons, for example. At the same time, the company also produces innovative and dramatic print designs using challenging images and scale to articulate the individuality, humour and boldness of both the company and the consumer. These appear to develop out of an eclectic and eccentric range of ideas and images, as described in Smith's publication, *You Can Find Inspiration in Everything*.

Timorous Beasties' printed textiles for the interiors market are mainly printed by hand in its Glasgow studio and sold via its two UK showrooms and an online site, along with Harrods, Liberty and other international outlets. Its imagery is largely based upon traditional references made contemporary through its use of scale, colour or adaptation.

While there are many differences between the designs of Paul Smith and Timorous Beasties, both design companies approach the printed image by referencing the history and heritage of

Top: Textile and wallcovering designs for contemporary interiors often use organic and naturalistic imagery. The unexpected twist – insect legs placed in a highly structured layout – is typical of Timorous Beasties' humorous approach to design.

Above: In the print for the 'Still Life – Rotten Fruit' shirt by Paul Smith, we can see photographic images of rotten fruit, used with consideration of scale, placement, tonal qualities and colour to create a dramatic and ethereal garment reminiscent of the paintings of Dutch Masters.

Left: In contrast to the shirt above, the 'Big Henry' print dress by Paul Smith shows a textural painted dress, dramatic in scale and colour.

art, design styles and printing technologies. They use image, scale, colour and method of application to the product or fabric to make these ideas contemporary and also relevant to their upmarket consumers, who have the confidence to wear or adorn their home with the dramatic, challenging printed images they produce.

The middle is the largest part of the marketplace, including some brands that have a distinct identity and appeal to a well-defined demographic, along with others with a more general approach that tend to be at the lower end of the middle market. The approach of mid-market brands and retailers is generally more focused on trend prediction than that of the higher end and, significantly, they will attempt to shape their own identity by interpreting a given trend into something to which their target consumer will respond positively. Another common feature of this level is flexibility, developing new product quickly as one trend supersedes another. The ability of a brand to understand and develop for its target consumer is paramount: two good examples are the international brands Ikea and Ted Baker.

Ikea is a global retailer situated towards the lower end of the middle market, with a clear product range aimed at a consumer who is interested in an economical and utilitarian approach to well-designed products for the home. It focuses on contemporary design using clean, modern lines in its products across all ranges.

The fashion company Ted Baker, also situated in the middle market, is characterized by fashion-forward design and a strong approach to print. Although a trend follower, it also has its own perspective on how to interpret and develop its collections. Its interpretation of 2010's floral trend is a good example, with a different look given to floral prints for a menswear shirt vs. a women's silk dress.

In the mass-market segment one of the largest retail brands is Walmart. In the UK it owns ASDA, which retails the George label of fashion and interior products. It has specific ranges aimed at different age groups, but essentially tries to capture a broad audience that appreciates trend-led imagery combined with competitively priced garments.

Walmart also offers a home range in the US and online, which includes bedding and other textile products designed to appeal to a wide range of price-conscious consumers, with variations including bold, bright, muted or monochrome colours; or floral, geometric, abstract, conversational, traditional or contemporary design styles.

Understanding the target consumer is imperative for a textile designer's awareness of market levels and requirements, and design decisions must be made from this perspective rather than from the designer's own preferences, as you will always be working either directly or indirectly for a company that has to respond to market needs. You should consider how this affects your interpretation or use of imagery, colour, materials and print heritage, and ultimately your design process.

Above: A dynamic and powerful pattern with a restrained colour palette uses bold and clean lines to communicate Ikea's contemporary style.

Right: Ted Baker's silk dress uses a painterly, softened and romantic interpretation of the floral trend, treating the dress as if it were an artist's canvas.

Anna Proctor, designer for a middle-market retailer, describes how quickly you learn the specifics of your market. She describes working with a design team developing womenswear, in which they were challenged to create new and aspirational designs to bring in new consumers without alienating their core customer. In the design studio and in meetings the customer was personalized as 'her' or 'she'. The team was encouraged to visit their flagship store regularly to look at the products and the customers. The leadership teams held 'huddles' that included presentations about their customers, their competitors and their market share, along with regular sales updates on products that succeeded or failed. Shopping trips to explore the ranges offered by competitors, as well as reporting back on alternative market approaches, were also very much encouraged.

Designers generally work in such teams, and the size of the organization is likely to dictate the number of people or departments. They may also liaise with technical areas and departments to support production and quality control, or collaborate with the fashion team to develop joint concepts for the next collection. Textile designers rarely work in isolation, and the ability to collaborate with others is an important skill to develop. Being able to share your views and be persuasive is important, as is accepting feedback and being open to ideas. You may find that 'team projects' are part of your textile design course, so that you can begin to acquire some of these skills.

You can investigate your target market in similar ways by considering one particular brand and its marketing approach in the retail environment and online. It is also important to consider a range of companies at a particular market level, analyzing what is different and/or similar about their approaches to design, print styles, fabric use and print processes, in order to build up a clearer understanding of the values of that level.

Above: Ted Baker interprets a floral trend for menswear in a bold and graphic way, with abstracted and simplified imagery that is layered with more complex shapes.

Right: ASDA's approach is one of fast-fashion, following trends closely with a quick turnaround of its textile-based products.

TREND PREDICTION

In the process of researching and developing your collection to resolve your design brief you must also be aware of the general zeitgeist, or spirit of the times, and the societal and cultural changes taking place that will influence what consumers want to buy when your designs are scheduled to reach the marketplace. Trend prediction is an industry that has developed to support designers, manufacturers and retailers in their decision-making processes.

Trend researchers may collect hard data from consumer and market research companies as well as news from 'cool hunters', looking at both the 'bubble-up' effect from emerging 'street fashion' and new cultural phenomena, and the 'trickle-down' effect from designers. Constantly on the lookout for the 'next thing', they will visit fashion weeks in major and emerging markets as well as design graduate shows and important art and museum exhibitions to pick up new ideas. They then analyze and assimilate their findings, arranging them into colour palettes, imagery and silhouettes in order to define a new zeitgeist that those in the industry use to inform the development of their collections for the new season.

The process typically begins two years in advance of the season, culminating in a package of information to offer guidance and analysis on the mood and direction of the market, including colours, materials, print direction, styling and images, consumers and technology. Trend predictors communicate with their clients through printed publications, online services and personal presentations. There are now many companies that offer web-based subscription services with information updated on a daily basis. Some of the organizations also do lecture tours to industry and universities.

While there are larger groups involved in trend prediction, such as Peclers Paris, Nelly Rodi, Carlin International, WGSN, Stylesight and Trendstop, there are also many smaller design studios producing bespoke trend packages for their clients. These packages are usually hand-rendered and presented with a more personal feel. In addition, some of the forecasting agencies have developed packages for niche markets such as lingerie or sportswear. WGSN or Trendstop, for example, offer a full fashion overview or the option to purchase a print and graphic prediction module only.

With some segments of the industry developing 'fast fashion', this has led to some changes in the turnaround time for apparel; within the middle and low market segments the two-season year has changed to one in which three ranges may be produced per season, or in some instances a new range every month. The emergence of Zara on the high street in the 1990s dramatically reduced the turnaround time for new ranges from six months to six weeks; it now claims to have reduced this process to two weeks. This has been enabled mainly by new technologies supporting faster production and 'leaner' supply chains, but it is also the result of Zara's 'local' manufacturing in Spain and Portugal, which provides the company with logistical

Chunky patterned knitwear

Arctic & alpine travel

A sense of escape & adventure

Textured & tonal graphics

Mudpie is one of the world's leading trend-forecasting companies and an internationally renowned authority on trend intelligence and design consultancy to the apparel, textile and creative industries. Its online service, MPDClick.com, provides creative trend intelligence to the world's most forward-thinking brands, and is the only global online trend service with a background in design.

flexibility. Decisions can be made quickly, replacing unpopular products with a constant flow of fresh on-trend merchandise.

The result of this constant turnover of products is the creation of ever-greater consumer demand. Part of this speeding up of the production cycle also stems from the reliance of the fashion industry on a system described as 'planned obsolescence'. Planned obsolescence encourages us to grow dissatisfied with what we already have – not because it has worn out, but because it is no longer fashionable. Therefore we begin a search for a new purchase that will lead us to be on trend again, and so the cycle continues.

While new merchandise is arriving in the shops ever more quickly, the consumer-led media has so far maintained a spring/summer and autumn/winter approach to merchandising, as this is how consumers still tend to think about their wardrobes. It is similar in interiors, where consumers look for advice about how to make the home cosy in winter and light and airy in summer.

However, planned obsolescence requires the industry to present a united approach to changing trends. This unity comes from the sources of information – the trend predictors – that are informing the manufacturing and retailing sector. Designers should interpret trend and prediction intelligence thoughtfully, enabling them to create lively, vibrant, innovative and interesting designs that are appropriate to the market for which they are designing.

Anna Proctor, a designer with a large high-street fashion retailer, states:

> Trend-prediction services are just part of how we pull together our ideas for the upcoming season; we look at catwalks, magazines, exhibitions, as well as shopping trips abroad and getting out in London regularly. We try and see design studios regularly to see the looks they are pushing as well as questioning them about what is selling . . . the important thing to remember is that they (trend predictions) are not a primary source . . . they can spark a really exciting idea but may also not be right for your brand. If you try and use them as your sole source of info and try to follow them too closely you may really struggle to make the concept work.

Trend magazines and other such resources are invaluable sources of visual inspiration for designers, providing timely trend information as well as a library for ideas in the future.

TRADE FAIRS

Trade fairs for fashion and textiles are held worldwide and are an important part of the process of trend development and prediction. Première Vision, an apparel fabric trade fair held in Paris in September and in February, has versions in New York, Shanghai, São Paulo, Moscow and Japan. For interiors there is Heimtextil, which is held in Frankfurt in January and also exhibits in Japan and Russia. Trade fairs are also organized to focus upon a particular group: they may be concentrated around a product type, such as yarns or lingerie; a particular market level, such as middle to high-end; links in the supply chain, such as dyeing and finishing; or a geographical area.

The purpose of attending trade fairs is to buy or sell products, build and/or maintain networks or relationships with suppliers and to gain information about trends, new products, processes, technologies and markets in order to keep up-to-date with industry changes. Most trade fairs, such as Première Vision, have an area specifically for the trade press and trend companies as well as their own trend forums for textiles and colours. Trade fairs are held from six to 18 months in advance of the season to which they relate.

Trade fairs often have an area for textile designers to sell their designs, and this is the main selling platform for many textile designers and design studios. At Première Vision there is a specific area called Indigo where textile designers sell their work, either as individuals, as studios or through an agent. Indigo holds similar interior events in Paris, Brussels and New York. Increasingly there have also been stands at Indigo that sell vintage or antique products, garments, samples, books and art.

Fashion weeks are also key events in the textile designer's calendar; designers attend the events themselves or follow the reports and images in the trade press, magazines, newspapers and on the Internet. The potential influence of key designers and the trends shown on the catwalks should be considered as part of a print designer's research and analysis.

Some trade fairs include a section where print studios can show buyers their latest design collections.

THE MEDIA

The media offers a wide range of resources to the designer: consumer magazines, trade press, newspapers, Internet, blogs and social networking sites can all assist you in your research of design inspiration, as well as in understanding changes in cultural, business and consumer trends.

Consumer magazines function as 'cultural intermediaries' between the industry and the public by promoting, advising and commenting on what and who is cool, and on how to put looks together.

Independent magazines, such as *NYLON* or *Amelia's Magazine*, present the edgier aspects of contemporary design and culture. These publications differ journalistically from the corporate style of the mass magazines, taking a more individual approach to fashion, music, art, design and other aspects of culture.

The trade press, now available in online versions, includes niche publications offering technical updates, information about how global events might be affecting the textile design industry, or business analysis about the industry. This insider's knowledge about your industry can also help in supporting your design strategy.

Newspapers often have style sections dedicated to fashion, design and culture, with information about upcoming events, designers and products. They may also review exhibitions and awards relevant to the industry.

Social networking sites and blogs offer the opportunity to participate in discussing and considering what to wear and how to put things together to create an individual 'look'. Bloggers also discuss interiors, documenting their redecorating schemes with accompanying photographs and images showing the inspiration behind their new colour palette.

The role of a textile designer is to mediate, analyze and connect a variety of influences to create a commercial design collection. Understanding the four design strands (design inspiration; design styles and print heritage; understanding the printed textile market; and trend prediction) that provide the context within which you will develop and resolve your collection will give you a sense of direction as you begin your research. Your approach to design inspiration, your interpretation of design styles and printing processes, along with your understanding of market segments and consumer trends, will grow with experience, allowing you to develop clearer strategies to capture exactly what you need from your visual resources.

Top and middle: An independent publication, *Amelia's Magazine* has a more individual and quirky style than many of the larger corporate publications. In its role as a cultural intermediary, it focuses upon creativity across art, design, fashion and music.

Above: Blogs allow each of us to become our own trendsetter or commentator, and enable designers to keep up with market trends in a wide range of products.

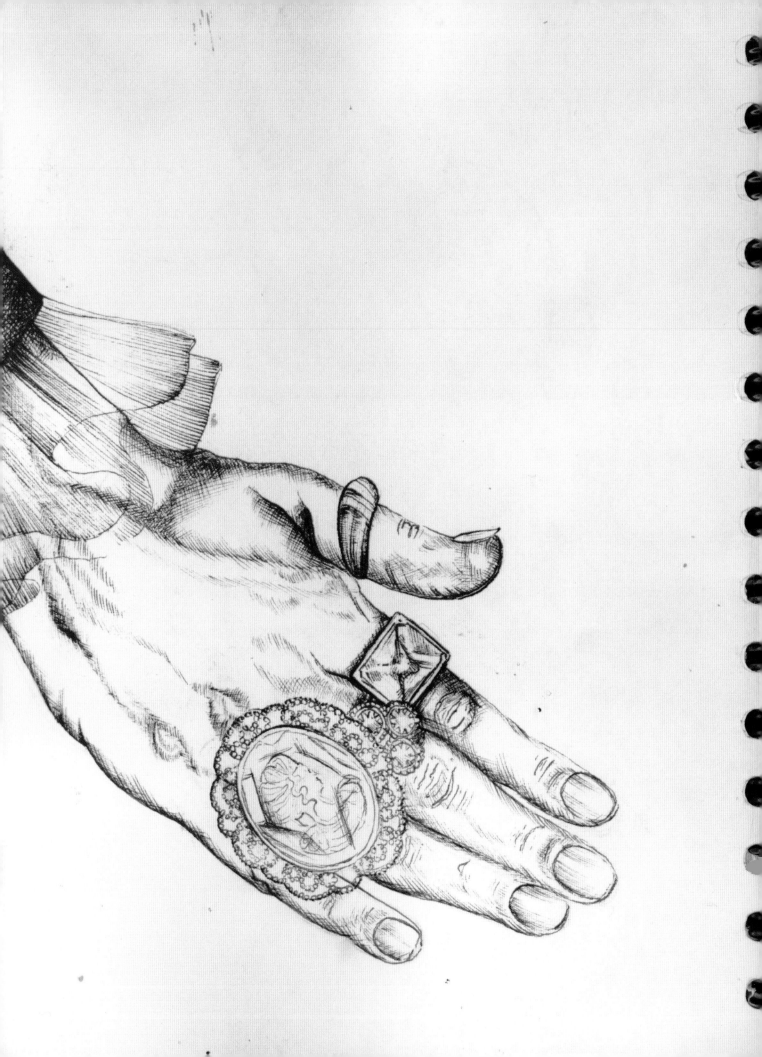

2
DESIGN
FUNDAMENTALS

INTRODUCTION
DESIGN FUNDAMENTALS

In the process of developing a collection of prints to resolve a design brief, the textile designer begins by synthesizing the elements of design inspiration, the heritage of print styles and processes and market levels and trend prediction, in the context of the brief's requirements. The designer must then employ a fundamental set of design skills to begin visual research, followed by design development that will lead to the physical reality of a textile design collection. This chapter will focus upon the design skills of drawing, colour use and repeat as tools for visual research, and will demonstrate that these skills are central to the successful practice of printed textile design.

The most basic of skills – drawing – enables you to initiate, explore, develop and resolve your design ideas. Drawing, or mark-making, is a broad term that can relate to collage or creating texture as much as it can to a linear drawing or brushwork. Drawing can be viewed as a spectrum from the representational to the totally abstract, and uses a wide range of media and substrates.

Understanding the principles of colour, as well as knowing how to use and develop colour palettes, are essential to the textile designer. Because our eye perceives and responds to the colour of a design, garment or product before we think about the imagery or texture, colour is a key driver for the sales of printed textiles.

Printed textile designers also need to understand how to design in repeat. Repeat is essentially the ability to reproduce exactly the same image over and over again, and attention is needed to ensure that the image will repeat precisely so that the pattern can be matched across the edges of the design, as well as being visually pleasing. The use of repeat is an industry requirement to enable efficient and economical manufacturing of both the printed cloth and its subsequent product application.

The use of repeat is also a design tool. Designers can exploit repeats to create a structured directional pattern, a multidirectional design, or a random appearance. If your design ideas rely on repetition or the impact of repeated pattern, then it is likely that you will be exploring repetition early on in design development. If your approach to repeat is for manufacturing purposes, however, then its consideration is likely to come later in the process.

This chapter outlines some of the strategies and approaches that you can follow as you begin your drawing process, start to apply colour theory and learn to use repeat as a design tool as well as to meet manufacturing requirements. Each of these skills will enable you to progress towards the development of your design collection and the resolution of your design brief.

Above: This seemingly traditional pattern by Paul Willoughby is made more contemporary by the insertion of incongruous motifs.

Previous pages: Drawing from life, as in this beautiful sketchbook example by Louise Coleman, provides an opportunity to understand the visual elements of an image while also creating mood through subject, medium and style.

Above left: Drawing and mark-making are essential skills for the textile designer, as illustrated in this fine pen drawing with colour wash by Jo Bedell.

Above: Drawing can capture line, contour, form, texture, negative space and colour, as in this observational drawing by Wendy Braithwaite.

Left: This abstract landscape painting by Phoebe Moss uses a muted colour palette to beautiful effect.

DRAWING

Drawing, painting and mark-making are the primary tools of the printed textile designer; enjoying the process of making marks on paper or fabric is intrinsic to the practice of this subject.

Your approach to drawing may be influenced by the heritage of particular print styles or processes, depending on the details of the brief. For example, if your brief asked you to consider botanical florals, your approach might be to consider very detailed drawings of an individual flower head. You might do some specific studies of the stamen or how the petals meet the stalk, perhaps using media that enables you to be precise. Alternatively, if you were asked to produce romantic florals, you might consider groups of flowers in bouquets and your interpretation might be softer and more fluid, using media that allows you to layer colour.

Drawing from life gives you the best opportunity to understand the visual elements of an image because you can study it from all angles; it is preferable to drawing from a photograph, which is only a flat representation of a scene. However, sometimes photography will enable you to capture images that you can then work on at a more appropriate time. Rather than confining yourself to drawing a single object, you might sometimes set up a group of objects to create a still life; or on occasion you might need to create something so that you can draw from it.

Similarly, you may be interested in capturing imagery from something more transient or ethereal, such as smoke or microscopic images. In these circumstances you would need to invest time and effort in devising ways to capture such imagery. There are no rules about how a drawing is created; some of the most exciting images might emerge from using odd tools or textures to draw or paint with, or from a combination of processes.

Printed textile designers draw either in a sketchbook or on loose sheets of paper and sometimes do both. Sketchbooks are often useful because you can keep them to hand in order to capture something that you see that is interesting or relevant to you at any moment. Drawing should enable you to study your object(s) and explore line, form, colour, scale, texture and surface qualities, allowing your own personal interpretation of the object to become evident. This initial exploration should employ a wide range of media to enable you to develop confidence and ability and to extend your skills. Drawing exercises can help you get to know the object and develop a strategy for your approach to it.

Above: Drawing is part of your visual research; it is a tool that enables you to capture information to support the development of the ideas evolved from studying a design brief. Zephyr Liddell's drawings demonstrate that simple use of line and mark, in this case combined with collage, can lead to sophisticated outcomes.

Below: Drawing is about looking at an object and trying to interpret it in a way that has some personal resonance, as well as moving towards the resolution of your design brief. Emma Shipley's highly naturalistic and detailed drawing reveals her personal approach.

WARM-UP EXERCISES

Begin with exercises that focus upon one element of the still life or object that you are drawing, such as line or form, using an appropriate medium. For instance, if you are considering line, use a line-making tool; to capture form, use charcoal or pastel so that you can create tones and shapes rather than lines. Then do some timed drawings – of one, three and then five minutes. Do not focus on creating fantastic drawings (though they might be) but think of it in the same way as waking up and stretching – these are just warm-ups to get you moving and thinking. Ask yourself what you want to capture from your subject. Why have you chosen to draw that object or items? What interests you about it? Do you want an abstract, a representational or an interpretational drawing style? What qualities of the object do you want to capture? Is there texture? Is it shiny, or highly detailed? What medium would best capture those qualities? How you choose to look at your objects will determine your approach to your drawing.

The ideas on the following pages will provide some suggestions for embarking on your visual research.

Above: In these timed one-, three- and five-minute drawings, charcoal has been used as a soft medium to capture the form of this flower head.

Below: A pencil captures the outline and beginnings of detail in these timed one-, three- and five-minute drawings of a plant.

EXERCISE 1
GET TO KNOW YOUR SUBJECT

You can try a range of approaches to gather information and develop ideas about your subject. You may initially have chosen something because you like the shape of it; be curious, studying it further to notice its texture, colour, surface effects, linear qualities, or how the lighting conditions create interesting shadows. You could also focus on the negative spaces it creates: the spaces around or within it.

◆ If an object is small, place it in a bag. Feel it and try to draw what you feel.

◆ Give someone directions on how to draw your object, or make your drawing as they direct you.

◆ Draw by guiding someone else's hand holding the medium. This forces you to think hard about how to capture the shape of the object, but may also create surprising effects.

◆ Use a magnifying glass.

◆ Draw your object reflected in a mirror.

◆ Curve, bend or distort one of your original drawings, and then draw from it.

◆ Place plastic or patterned glass in between you and your object.

Left: Francesca Caputo uses a range of thick painterly marks to attempt to capture the depth and textural surface qualities of this flower.

Below: Using a pencil to draw this group of fish, Elissa Bleakley captures individual details as well as considering the composition of the subjects.

Bottom: Sarah Patterson's collection uses architectural imagery – beginning her research with simple paper stencils and photographing them in subdued lighting to create dramatic urban landscapes that will inspire her drawings.

EXERCISE 2
DRAWING WITH LINE

You can approach drawing using linear qualities with the following ideas:

◆ **Work with the wrong hand.**

◆ **Attach a brush or pencil to a long stick.**

◆ **Draw in candlelight.**

◆ **Using a ruler, draw only with straight lines.**

◆ **Experiment with different tools or pressure to create unique linear qualities.**

Left: Drawing and painting by candlelight, Bethany Holmes captures a soft and fluid impression of these flowers.

Below centre: Jo Bedell uses a linear approach to create a representational and atmospheric drawing of a face, while tone and shade are used to create depth.

Below left: Holly Betton uses a free, painterly approach to capture the spirit of subjects.

Bottom centre: Rachel Harris combines charcoal lines with paint to create a simplified and textural interpretation of a floral motif.

Below right: Alex MacNaughton's drawings of birds show an interest in an illustrative style and use of stitching on a domestic machine as a method of creating texture and surface effects.

EXERCISE 3
DRAWING FORM

Trying to capture the subtlety of form by using tonal qualities to shade and suggest depth is a more challenging approach. It is usually best to attempt this by using media that limit your ability to create line – usually soft or wet media such as charcoal, pastels or paint. You need to draw by looking only at the form of the object, resisting the desire to draw a line or focus on the contours of the object.

- ◆ Use soft or wet media – charcoal, pastels or paint.

- ◆ Think about the material or composition of the object.

- ◆ Work from positive to negative by covering a whole sheet of paper in charcoal and then using an eraser to draw by removing areas of charcoal.

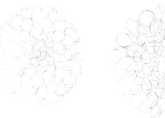

Left: In this page from Lucinda Dann's sketchbook she first sketches the linear shape of a flower head, then adds colour and tone to capture the full depth of the flower.

Below left: Jo Bedell captures the form of the horse's head by using white, grey and black pastels to build up depth.

Below right: Bethany Holmes uses paint in gradations of colour to capture depth and form in this simple floral image.

EXERCISE 4
DRAWING TEXTURE

Texture can be created by drawing detail or by mark-making with your choice of media. You can also create a textural effect by using collage, or by drawing over a textured surface that can be exposed by working onto it with a soft medium, such as charcoal.

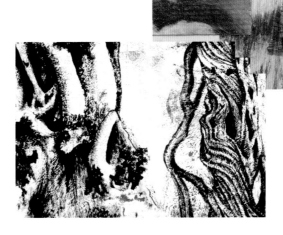

- ◆ Textures can be created by using media that create textural marks when you are drawing – such as charcoal or chalk.

- ◆ Textures can also be created by using resists, such as wax or masking fluid. Cutting, folding, tearing, creasing or crumpling papers can also texturize your image.

- ◆ Photocopying the same image repeatedly can degrade the qualities of the drawing and thus can create textures.

- ◆ Use thick paint into which you can then make marks.

- ◆ Using a range of surfaces to draw upon can create unusual effects. Try drawing on papers or plastics, or paint on a mirror or other reflective surface.

- ◆ Use sources such as found paper to collage with; try absorbent papers with thin materials.

- ◆ Use bleach to remove the colour from previously painted or treated surfaces.

Above: Nahim Akhtar uses a variety of media, including oil pastels and charcoal, to create a range of textures and form.

Above left: Here Jo Bedell has used distressed and crumpled paper to create textured qualities with paint and line drawing.

Left: Using collage as a mechanism to explore landscape in an abstract way, Phoebe Moss creates a range of surface qualities through the use of paper, card, tape and paint.

Below left: Painting on unusual surfaces can create exciting effects; here, Emma Wolf uses an absorbent paper to capture the soft and fluid marks of the feathers.

Below: Jessica Beavis has scored marks in thickly applied paint on paper to create these textural effects.

COLOUR

Colour is a vital component of a printed textile design – it helps to convey the mood and connect the designs within your collection. The study of colour theory is important for all art and design subjects; it enables you to understand how colour works and how to mix colours using paint or on a computer. You will also need to consider how colours work together in a collection, taking into account colour forecasting and cycles, as well as their appropriateness for the products or market segment for which you are designing.

COLOUR THEORY

Colour theory has been the subject of scientific and cultural enquiry for many centuries. In the seventeenth century, Sir Isaac Newton was the first to identify the colour spectrum of red, orange, yellow, green, blue, indigo and violet that could be seen when light passed through a prism. Other theorists, including Johann Wolfgang von Goethe and Michel Eugène Chevreul, both working in the nineteenth century, focused upon understanding our perceptions of colour.

In the twentieth century artists and designers began to develop theories about colour and its use within the visual arts. Johannes Itten and Josef Albers taught colour at the Bauhaus design school; Itten's *The Art of Color* and Albers's *Interaction of Color* remain important texts on colour theory for artists and designers. Colour theory includes two systems of understanding colour: additive and subtractive, depending on whether colour is seen as light, or as pigment on a surface. Subtractive colour is the process of mixing pigments; as colours are added to a white ground, more light is absorbed and less is reflected, hence the term 'subtractive'.

The subtractive primary colours of red, blue and yellow can't be created from other colours, but are used to create all other colours. Secondary colours are produced by mixing two primaries together (red + blue = violet), while tertiary colours are created by mixing a primary with its adjacent secondary (red + violet = red violet).

If red, blue and yellow are mixed together in equal quantities a pure black should result; however, due to the imperfections in pigments it is likely that a muddy brown would emerge instead.

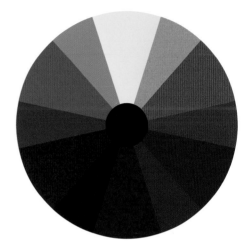

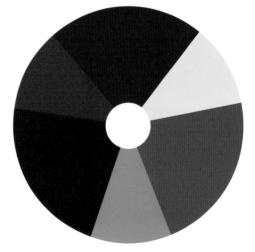

Top: Subtractive colours are seen as pigments on a surface; when combined they move towards black, as less light is reflected. The subtractive colour wheel places the primaries of red, blue and yellow in a triangular relationship, with the secondary and tertiary colours in between.

Below: The additive primary colours, or colours of light, are red, green and blue; when combined in equal proportions they create white. Both the subtractive and additive colour wheels position colours opposite their complementaries.

Additive colour is the process of mixing coloured *light* together, and we see this in action on a TV screen or on a computer monitor. When the additive primaries of red, green and blue are combined, the resulting secondary colours are cyan, magenta and yellow – different from the secondary colours created when the subtractive primaries are mixed (orange, green and violet).

This will explain why what you see on your computer monitor can differ from what you see printed on either paper or fabric. Subtractive and additive colour have different mixing systems with different primary colours; therefore the printed form of an image will appear more dull than the on-screen version. Textile software programmes generally incorporate a colour management system to help you minimize these screen/print discrepancies.

When the design is placed in the manufacturing process the responsibility for colour accuracy passes to colourists in the laboratory or printing plant. Colour management is, therefore, very important in order to ensure colour consistency across a product range, and there are a number of colour systems designed to communicate colour accurately. One such system is Pantone®, which enables you to match a colour to a specified and coded colour library. Use of such a system with a specific colour vocabulary enables those involved in the manufacturing process to ensure colour accuracy.

Digital design programs can create problems with colour accuracy because the relationships between monitors, software and printers are so variable. To minimize this problem, digital fabric printers usually hold a colour library that can be used to match your colour requirements. Each colour in the library has an associated set of values that you can check your colours against; when you have decided which is the right one you can input these values into your design. However, it is wise to print off colour swatches on more than one type of fabric so that you can double-check colours prior to putting in a large print order, as the fibre content of a fabric will affect the way in which it takes colour.

Top: This is a section taken from a digital printer colour library. You can use this library to ensure colour accuracy when printing digitally on different fabrics by checking the code for each colour that you wish to use.

Bottom: After printing a range of design samples, Jessica Beavis checks them against her colour standards to ensure colour accuracy.

Colour has its own specific vocabulary, which you need to understand in order to communicate as your design collections develop. Often food or other types of natural objects become references that we use to communicate colour to each other. Designers use other words to create a mood or atmosphere when describing colour. We might describe a particular brown as being 'chocolate' brown to distinguish it from one with a more ochre hue, as in the pair of browns shown below. Alternatively we might use the term 'lime green' as opposed to 'pea green', or 'chilli red' as opposed to 'blood red'.

Terms such as acid, pastel, jewel tone or fluorescent may not necessarily be accurate, but are still useful design references. Equally, periods of time may help to describe a colour – a '1930s look' may be used in a design brief to explain the mood communicated by a subdued, dulled-out colour palette.

In this Marimekko print 'Tuliainen' by Pia Holm, hot orange is used in small proportion as a highlight colour and adds warmth to the cool, muted palette.

Chocolate Ochre

Pastel

Lime Pea

Jewel tone

Chilli Blood

1930s

COLOUR DEFINITIONS

However, as a designer it is important to utilize a more precise colour vocabulary in order to achieve and communicate the various levels of colour and nuances of mood required in your designs. You should understand the following terms:

Hue: another word for colour.

Value: the amount of light or dark in a colour; a colour with a high amount of white has a high value.

Chroma: the amount of a pure colour present; absence of grey.

Saturation: the intensity of a colour, similar to chroma. Below is a colour at full intensity and at different levels of desaturation.

Temperature: a colour is classified as 'warm' when it is mixed with red, orange or yellow, or is considered 'cool' when mixed with green, blue or violet. A good exercise to explore colour temperature uses the primary and secondary colours on the subtractive colour wheel (see page 46). Divide a primary colour in two, add its right-hand neighbour to one half and then its left-hand neighbour to the other. Adding orange to red will make it appear a little warmer (red-orange); adding violet will make it appear cooler (red-violet), as below.

Contrast: the tonal differences between colours.

Simultaneous contrast: the perception that a colour is altered when used against the colour adjacent to its complement on the subtractive colour wheel; a colour will lend its adjacent colour a complementary tinge. Violet seen against orange will have a blue cast, as blue is the complement of orange. If violet is seen against green it will appear more red as this is the complement to green.

Examining how colour is used trains the eye to consider proportions and combinations. Look at contrasting or harmonious relationships, or the mood conveyed by the palette, in a fabric you admire. In 'Toria' by Liberty Art Fabrics, a close colour palette is used, relying on tints to create harmony alongside a contrasting white and taupe.

Saturation

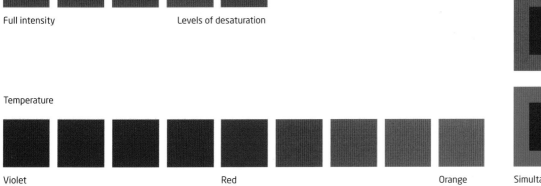

Full intensity   Levels of desaturation

Temperature

Violet   Red   Orange   Simultaneous contrast

Tint: a colour with the addition of white.

Shade: a colour with the addition of black.

Tone: a colour with the addition of grey.

Highlight colour: a hue used in a small proportion to create a visual lift.

Naturals: colours that are evocative of natural qualities (sky, earth, water).

Neutrals: muddy or earthy colours made up of multiple complementaries; because the components are not 100 per cent pure, they create a neutral colour rather than black.

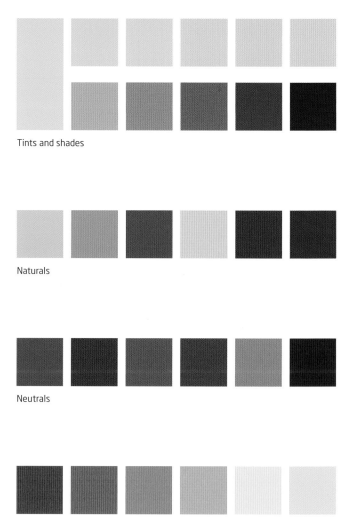

Tints and shades

Naturals

Neutrals

Harmonious colours or colour schemes: colours used in relationships that are pleasing to the eye. While colours can be combined in infinite variations of hues, tints, shades and tones, harmonious relationships are likely to be one of the following:

Analogous colours

◆ **Analogous colours:** close together on the subtractive colour wheel.

◆ **Monochromatic colours:** tints or shades of the same hue.

Monochromatic colours

◆ **Complementary hues:** colours directly opposite one another on the colour wheel; complementary colours are red and green, yellow and violet, blue and orange.

◆ **Split complementaries:** using a hue with the two hues on either side of its complementary colour. For example, red would be used with blue-green and yellow-green, the colours either side of red's complementary, which is green.

Split complementaries

◆ **Harmonious triads:** three hues or colours equally spaced around the subtractive colour wheel.

◆ **Tetradic colour schemes:** linking two complementary or split complementary colours. These schemes are complex and work best if one colour dominates and the other hues have altered values.

Harmonious triads

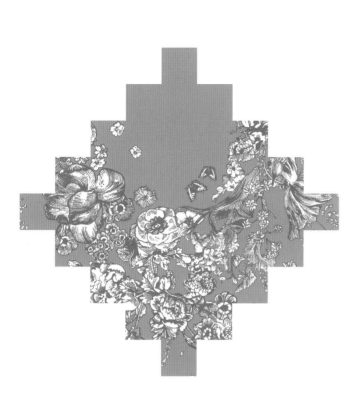

Above left: This Cole and Son design from the 'Fornassetti' collection uses a monochromatic palette.

Above right: This dress from Erdem's spring/summer 2010 collection features a monotone palette of tints, tones and shades.

Far left: Erdem's collection for autumn/winter 2011/12 used a harmonious colour palette restricted to tones of autumnal reds, oranges, browns and black.

Left: Alexander McQueen utilizes neutrals – muddy or earthy tones – in this camouflage rose dress.

COLOUR PALETTES

The building of a colour palette for your design collection will be affected by a number of factors: a blend of influences from your drawing and visual research, the printing method you wish to use, and the season, predictions, trends and market level for which you are designing. Alternatively, the colour palette may have been identified in the design brief. A colour palette might typically consist of around 12 colours, but there are no hard and fast rules.

Each design within a collection needs to have a different 'feel', and colour can assist in creating designs that conjure different atmospheres. At the same time, your collection requires a sense of cohesion, and your colour palette is one factor that enables you to achieve this. How you use this palette is your choice – some designs may use two colours and others may have eight.

While the colours we choose in our apparel and our homes reflect our personal tastes, it is important to recognize that as a designer you will be expected to work with varying ranges of colours and combinations that are not necessarily your favourites. You might find that you have a selection of colours that you use more often and feel comfortable with; if so, make a conscious effort to consider a broader colour palette.

You should also be aware that colour has symbolic meanings in different cultures and their rituals. At a wedding in Western culture, for example, the bride wears white; but at many Asian weddings a bride wears red. In the West black is often associated with death, while in parts of Asia white is associated with mourning.

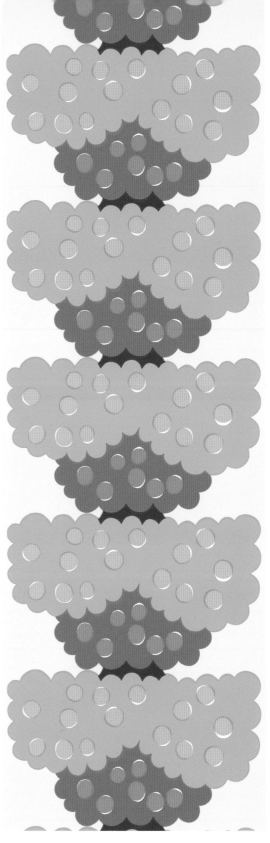

Above: The colour palette of yellow and yellow-cast greens creates a fresh, spring feeling in the abstract print 'Max and Moritz' designed for Marimekko by Maija and Kristina Isola.

Left: This muted colour palette by Angie Lewin for St Jude's is reminiscent of the 1950s.

The colour palette for your design collection may be inspired by your research or by trend forecasts, or it may be identified in the design brief. Xiao Wang has expressed her colour palette in her sketchbook drawings.

COLOUR PROPORTIONS

Begin to invesitgate a colour palette from your visual research by painting out some flat colour on A4 or A3 sheets of paper. It is then easy to cut out small squares, or chips, at the same size so that you can view them in equal proportions and evaluate them. It is also useful to cut out strips of varying widths of each of the colours you have chosen and place them together in groups as stripes.

It is easy to do the same thing digitally, using a drawing package to build a colour palette that you can then explore simply by playing around with strips of colour. Whichever way you choose to create your palette, you should learn to evaluate colour combinations and proportions so that you can begin to introduce them to your design development.

Textile designs for interior collections often demand that you consider a range of colourways. You should spend some time looking at interior fabric swatch books or interior collections online to understand how a palette may be applied through several different colourways. It is also interesting to note the impact of colour on each version of the design: which elements move forward, which disappear and which elements appear in the positive or negative space.

The way a colour palette is developed may also depend on the technical requirements of the printing method. In screen printing each separate colour requires its own screen, adding cost and time to the process. While six to eight colours are commonly used in prints for fashion and interiors, some high-end fabrics, particularly those for interiors, might use up to 24 colours. On the other hand, digital printing has no colour limits because each colour can be created from the four to eight inkjet colours available.

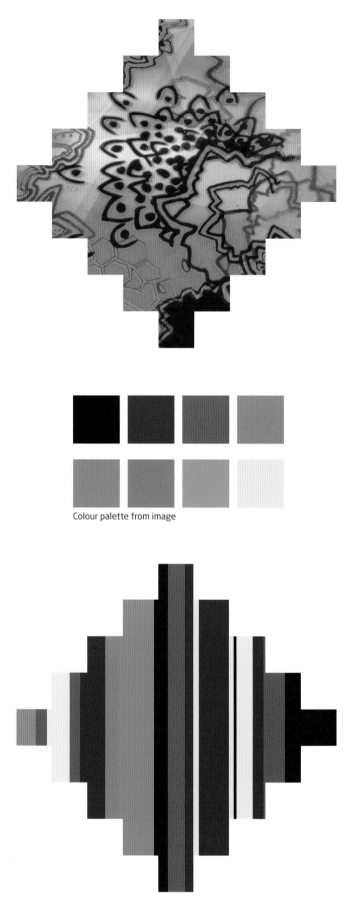

Colour palette from image

When experimenting with a new palette, evaluate the effects of colour and proportion to understand which combinations work, and why.

COLOUR CYCLES

If we consider the way in which colour palettes change in fashion we might notice that they tend to evolve and develop in cycles rather than being overthrown each season. Within a seasonal palette there may be long-term core colours, long-term fashion colours and short-term fashion colours. Long-term core colours are usually classics such as white, black, navy, beige and grey. Mid-term fashion colours tend to have an impact for several seasons and may be identified as a group, such as deep reds. The short-term fashion colours, which change more frequently, may last for only one season; these tend to be bolder and more impactful.

Colour forecasters develop seasonal colour palettes, using trend research to develop these short-term colours and fitting them alongside the colours with a longer lifecycle. It is these short-term colours and their rate of change that help to drive the planned obsolescence of the fashion industry.

Using a similar approach when developing your own palette, think about your colours in groups. You might start with a selection of neutral or classic shades, and mid- and deeper tones for your fashion colours. Or you might add a group of bright accent shades. Adding breadth to a palette enables you to explore a range of visual effects, such as depth or intensity, to create complex or simple designs.

The cyclical nature of colour trends, along with the target market for your designs and the printing methods you choose, will influence your use of colour in building a palette for your design project. However, it is the understanding of colour theory that lies at the heart of your ability to interpret your design inspiration in saleable colourways.

This interior fabric, 'Viaduct' by Imogen Heath, uses long-, mid- and short-term colour trends. Her use of navy and black as the predominant colours ensures a strong, classic feel. Warm greys and taupes, which have had a strong appeal for several seasons in interiors, place it in the mid-term category. The use of 'nude', however, fits with current short-term colour trends.

REPEAT

One of the most important technical parameters in commercial textile printing is repeat, or the repetition of a pattern along the length and width of the fabric in mathematical precision. Many designers, particularly those working in design studios for fashion, may not consider repeat in a technical way at all, although designs for interior textiles are nearly always created in repeat. However, even if your designs are not going to be completed in repeat it is important that you are aware of the visual impact of repeat on your design and consider the continuity of the image across the edges of the design, as this gives an indication of the repeat. If the design is not in repeat, the retailer or the manufacturer will ensure that the repeat is completed prior to production by technicians in the design studio.

Motif and elements

More importantly, repeat is also a compositional tool allowing you to develop the designs you have been creating. When thinking about repeat, you need to consider whether you wish to develop a motif-based design or whether you would like to create a more complex image with a range of visual elements. Very few textile designs actually use a single motif; while one motif can create a very strong design statement, using several individual elements will result in a more complex and sophisticated design resolution.

Multidirectional design

In general terms, a single design tends to be composed of a range of visual elements developed through scale, media, colour and texture. It is important to remember when using a motif for repeat that it is actually the square space including the design that becomes the repeat, not the motif itself. You might also consider what kind of rhythm and flow you would like to create in your design through the structure of the repeat.

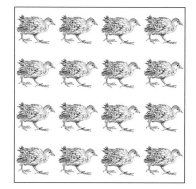

Block repeat

Most commercial textile designs are produced to be printed in repeat onto rolls of fabric that are relatively large. A rotary screen is 64cm (25in) in circumference and therefore 64 x 64cm (25 x 25in) or 32 x 32cm (12½ x 12½in) repeats are standard. With the increased use of digital design it is also common for designs for fashion to be printed on A4-sized paper, which is standard letter paper 210 x 297mm (8 x 11½in) or A3 paper, which is double A4, 420 x 297mm (16 x 11½in). Digital, or inkjet, printing can also be used to produce non-repeating patterns, engineered prints and patterns that are printed directly on fabric shapes or garments.

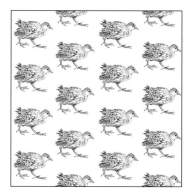

Half-drop

The repeat of pattern has its own vocabulary, which you need to be able to articulate and understand:

Motif and elements – these are the components that you use to build your design. A design may be made of one motif or several different elements.

Multidirectional design – this design works from any direction so as not to indicate a top or a bottom.

Block repeat – this is the repetition of a design in a grid-like structure. Some designs use the structure in an intentionally obvious manner, while skilled designers can make this simple pattern repeat difficult to spot.

Half-drop – this is also referred to as a step repeat, as it resembles a series of steps. The convention is that the 'drop' of the step will be half the size of the design, but it can as easily be a quarter or third. The half-drop is probably the most popular repeat and creates a less obvious repetition of the design, giving a more organic flow.

Brick repeat – this type of repeat looks like the standard brick formation you might expect to see in buildings.

Turnover repeat – in this repeat the element or motif is flipped along both the vertical and horizontal axes, creating a pattern mirroring effect in both directions.

Mirror repeat – an element or motif is flipped across its horizontal or vertical axis, creating an apparent mirror of itself. The ease of completing this type of pattern digitally has led to a glut of these designs appearing in recent years.

Spot repeat – also known as sateen repeat, this type of repeat often has a single or limited number of motifs or elements designed to appear random and multidirectional within a square. The square is then repeated as either block or half-drop.

There are other variations of repeat that you might come across, such as stripe, diamond, tossed, ogee, pillar and serpentine. Have a look around your home and wardrobe, or visit your local high street or a shopping mall to identify a variety of pattern repeats.

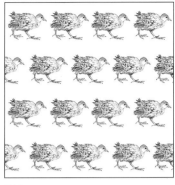

Brick repeat

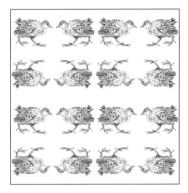

Turnover repeat

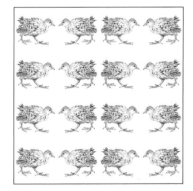

Mirror repeat

Spot repeat

COMMON PROBLEMS WITH REPEAT DESIGNS

Putting a design in repeat that has not been thoroughly thought through will result in the amplification of any mistakes, as they will be repeated across a whole width of fabric. Some mistakes are common: strong horizontals, verticals or diagonals can emerge from a composition when motifs have been inadvertently placed in a line; 'tramlines' can appear as a linear space around the design if you do not think carefully about working across the repeat; or ungainly spaces can emerge if you do not consider the composition sufficiently during the design process.

With enough practice, however, you can avoid these types of problem. When you are working on the screen and only looking at one view of your design, however, it can often be hard to spot any potential problems, so it helps to design in multiples at the same time. Digital methods make it particularly easy to repeat motifs and place these copies in each of your multiples simultaneously.

CREATING REPEATS WITH MULTIPLE MOTIFS

When you are starting to develop designs with multiple motifs it is a good idea to try and work in a way that enables you to work on a multiple of the design at the same time, allowing you to see what happens as it repeats. It is important that one motif does not dominate the design and that you consider the negative space of the overall image as you place each motif within the design space.

Looking at printed textile designs will show you that, while powerful and dramatic designs can be built using one single motif, most designs have several different motifs in them, which means that they appear less regimented and structured. Adopting this approach will enable you to develop more creative designs. You can practise by using paper and black-and-white photocopies to see what happens when you start placing motifs in repeat but you can also do this digitally by copying and pasting imagery.

These images show several of the stages of decision-making that the designer went through from the starting motifs to the finished design. The designer began with a 32 x 64cm (12½ x 25in) rectangle and worked in half-drop.

Above: In these three images individual motifs are being explored and placed within the design, with the scale, direction and colour of the birds being varied.

Below: These two images show the development of a background onto which the birds are going to be placed.

Left: Here some of the individual motifs are being placed to see how they interact with the background in order to arrive at a final composition and consider the colour balance.

Below: The final design in repeat uses a sinuous stripe of flowers moving vertically with the birds facing different directions. In some cases the birds are merged with the foliage. Their different scales, colours and directions, and the fact that the design is in half-drop, give the design a fluid visual feel.

PUTTING THEORY INTO PRACTICE

It is a good idea to become confident and fluent with repeat, trying out both manual and digital methods for putting designs into repeat. Have a look through your drawings or design ideas and decide on some motifs or elements of your work that you could attempt to develop into a repeat.

Using digital repeat methods is both quicker and easier than manual and it is rare that you will be expected to repeat a design manually. However, gaining an understanding of principles by constructing a repeat manually embeds the concept in your thinking and enables you to apply the understanding to digital methods.

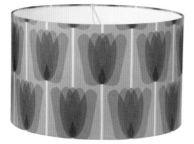

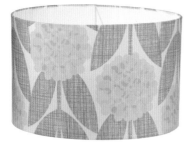

Top: This 'Pop Floral' motif by Aimee Wilder is made all the more dynamic by the use of a half-drop repeating structure.

Above left: The use of a brick repeat adds an interesting dimension to Wilder's quirky yet simple two-colour 'Sumo' design.

Above: Orla Kiely's 'Car Park' print relies on the balance between the dense background colour and the negative space of the car shape in this contemporary graphic design.

Left: Jane Gordon Clark uses negative space to organize leaf motifs in her wallpaper patterns, allowing the simplicity and understated qualities of the leaf to be the focus of the design.

Far left: This row of fabric lampshades demonstrates that motif repetition in a vertical or horizontal drop is a powerful tool. Orla Kiely uses single motifs with creativity and ease.

CREATING REPEATS BY HAND

You can either use tracing paper to copy ideas or you can use a photocopier to copy the motifs, marks or images with which you would like to experiment, working with a grid of 32cm (12½in) square and a motif of 8cm (3in) so that it can be repeated four times in both directions.

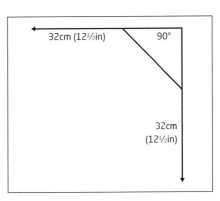

STEP 1
From the images that you have identified as being appropriate to use, identify one that you think could be useful as an individual motif.

STEP 2
Draw in pencil a 32cm (12½in) square, ensuring the corners are drawn at 90 degrees; use a set square if necessary.

STEP 3
Draw a grid, in dashed pale-pencil line, to enable you to place your motifs accurately. This grid should be relevant to the scale of your motif, so, for instance, if you drew your grid at 8cm (3in) intervals in both directions and your motif was 4cm (1½in) then each motif would have a 4cm (1½in) space between them.

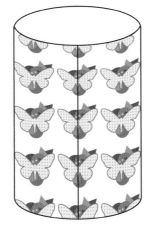

STEP 4
Using your tracing or photocopy, arrange your motif within this block nine times, at the intersection of each dashed line, so that the organization of the motif will create a grid-like pattern. Where the dashed lines meet the edges of the square only half of your motif will appear; there will be 12 of these. In the four corners you would place a quarter of the motif.

STEP 5
To prove or test the continuity of the design, cut the square to the edge and roll it into a tube. The elements should meet at the edges.

CAD REPEATS

Developing repeats through CAD (computer-aided design) systems gives you good resolution and also allows you to move into more intricate repeats. Some textile-specific software systems enable you to develop your design in repeat as you work. You can also complete repeat in standard off-the-shelf drawing packages such as Photoshop® Creative Suite 5 (used in the exercises below), adapting and inverting options that already exist. However, there are also textile-specific programs available – for example, AVA or Lectra's Kaledo software offer CAD solutions to textile design manufacturing requirements.

STEP BY STEP 2
SIMPLE MOTIF BLOCK REPEAT

In this exercise we are going to produce a design that requires a motif to be repeated in a simple block formation.

STEP 1
Choose a motif that has a solid colour or transparent background and decide the scale at which the motif would best work in relation to the design size. You can alter the size of the motif by going to **Image > image size**. This image was scaled to 2 x 2cm (¾ x ¾in).

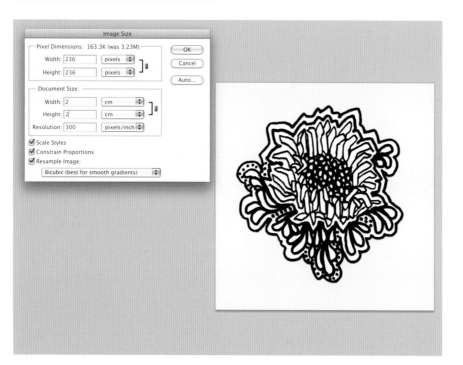

STEP 2

Give your motif a name in **Edit > define pattern**.

STEP 3

Open a new document, remembering to increase the dimensions to allow the image to be repeated – in this case we increased it to 10 x 10cm (4 x 4in), in which to place your motif: **Edit > fill**.

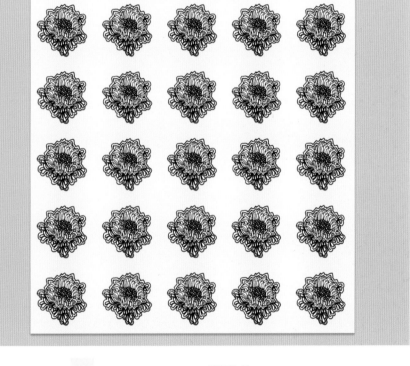

STEP 4

In the dialogue box that appears, select **pattern** and then a **custom pattern** box appears; click on this box and you should be able to see your saved motif.

IF YOU CAN SEE ONLY A SECTION OF YOUR MOTIF, IT IS PROBABLY TOO BIG FOR THE DIMENSIONS OF THE DOCUMENT IN WHICH YOU ARE REPEATING IT.

STEP 5

Select **OK** and your motif will appear repeated in the new document.

BLOCK REPEAT USING THE OFFSET FILTER

If you are working on a design idea that you would like to put into repeat, perhaps with a textured background, using the **offset filter** will allow you to integrate the pattern at the edges to create a continuous design free of visible joins. This process can often be time-consuming but results in a textile design that has image continuity in all directions.

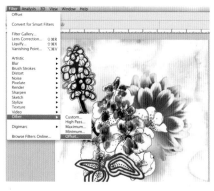

STEP 1
Begin by using the **offset filter**, which will divide the design into quarters and reconfigure them so that the external edges now appear as a cross in the centre: **Filter > other > offset**.

STEP 2
In the offset palette dialogue box ensure that **Wrap Around** is selected. To ensure that external edges appear as a cross in the centre of the design, divide the horizontal and vertical pixel image sizes in half, enter the new values and click **OK**. (You can check the size of the design by going to **Image > image size** and noting the pixel dimensions.)

STEP 3
You should now see the cross in the centre of the design where your image does not join. It is this area that you need to modify so that the edges disappear and the image looks integrated and continuous. Use any drawing and painting tools that feel appropriate; you can also use copy and paste and the clone brush if they help.

STEP 4

Photoshop works on a process of building up layers of images (try and think of it as a series of pieces of tracing paper). This is really useful when designing, as you can work on individual motifs separately without changing everything; however, when you are repeating it becomes complex. Therefore it is important to ensure that you don't build up layers at this point; if you do, you need to 'flatten' them into a single layer by using **Layer > flatten image**.

STEP 5

When you think you have completed your work on the edges, repeat the offset process so that you can check that there are no remaining edges.

STEP 6

When you feel you have a completely continuous image, you can go through the process of block repeating your pattern as in Step by Step 2: Simple Motif Block Repeat. Simply follow that process, remembering to increase the size of the new document relative to the size of the image you will be using.

HALF-DROP REPEAT

If you need to develop a design that is more complex than a half-drop repeat with a single motif – perhaps one that has a textured background – then you will need to put the whole design into half-drop. In order to do this digitally you will need to use the offset filter, which will allow you to manipulate the edges to work together. This process is complex and can be very time-consuming but the result is a textile design that has image continuity and also the more naturalistic visual qualities that emerge with this type of repeat.

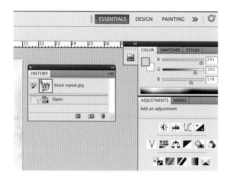

STEP 1
Ensure that your chosen image has had all of its layers flattened (**Layer > flatten image**) and then select **View > snap to > all**.

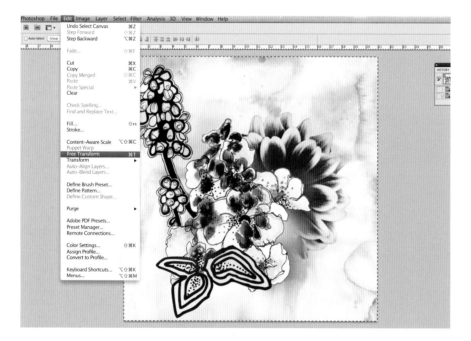

STEP 2
Click on **Edit > free transform**. When you do this, a small circle with crosshairs on it will appear in the middle of your window.

STEP 3
Now click on the **ruler** on the top of your window and drag down a guide so that it is touching the crosshairs in the middle of your screen (if you have **Snap to guides** selected you should find it easy).

STEP 4

Press the **escape** button on your keyboard, then **Select > all** your design and **Edit > copy**. Then **Select > deselect** your design.

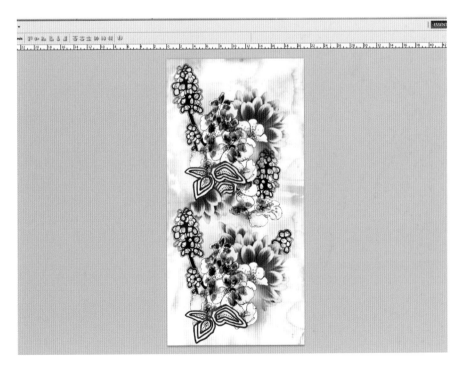

Canvas Size

Current Size: 17.6M
Width: 21 cm
Height: 21 cm

OK
Cancel

New Size: 35.2M
Width: 100 percent
Height: 200 percent
☐ Relative
Anchor:

Canvas extension color: Other...

STEP 5

Now you need to change the canvas size. Select **Image > canvas size**, select the bottom-middle square and change the height to **200 percent**; click **OK** and you will see that the canvas size has doubled in height.

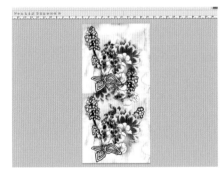

STEP 6

Click on **Edit > paste** and your image should appear; place it carefully in the space on the canvas: **Layer > flatten image**.

STEP 7

You should now see the join between the two copies of the design. You need to work on the joins to ensure that the edges disappear and that the image looks integrated and continuous. Use any drawing and painting tools that feel appropriate; you can also use copy and paste and the clone brush. Copying and pasting elements of the design can also ensure that you cover the join; be careful that you do not build up layers with this process. Use the eyedropper tool to ensure careful colour matching, and remember to save regularly.

STEP 8

Select > all and **Edit > copy**.

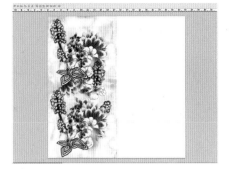

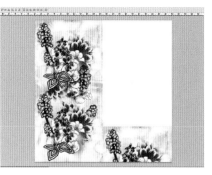

STEP 9

Select **Image > canvas size** and the left-hand middle square. Change the width to **200 percent**, click **OK**; the canvas will now have doubled in width.

STEP 10

Select **Edit > paste** and move the pasted image into the blank space to the right of the canvas and below the guide line.

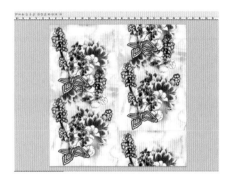

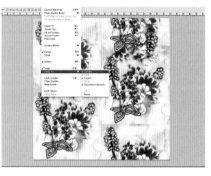

STEP 11

Edit > paste again and move this image into the blank space next to the image on the screen, this time above the guide line. Make sure all the layers are flattened: **Layer > flatten image**.

STEP 12

Select **View menu > deselect snap to guides** and deselect **show guides**.

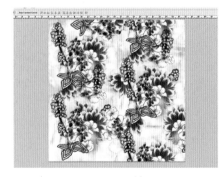

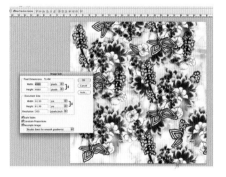

STEP 13

You should now see the joins in the design, so, as before, modify these edges to ensure that the image looks integrated and continuous.

STEP 14

Select **Image > image size** and note the pixel size.

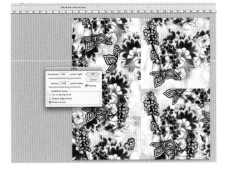

STEP 15

Select **Filter > other > offset**, making sure that **Wrap Around** is selected. Halve the pixel size of the design and note these numbers. It is likely that this might show further joins that you may need to work on.

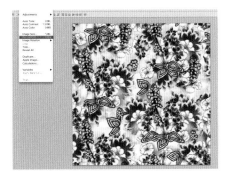

STEP 16

Select **Image > canvas size**, then select the bottom-middle square and change height to **50 percent.**

STEP 17

The design is now in a half-drop unit. You can fill it into any shape or size for printing on paper or fabric.

The best examples of repeat are without elements that seem to 'jump out' at you, or obvious gaps or 'tramlines' where the edges of the design meet. Understanding the basic principles of repeat, and learning to manipulate repeats both manually and digitally will allow you to explore and develop repeats as a creative tool and ensure that your repeats are 'seamless'. Through practice, you will build up these skills and be able to develop more sophisticated repeats.

Understanding the principles and learning the skills of drawing, colour and repeat are fundamental to becoming a practising textile designer. Mastering these fundamentals will help you to develop your design inspiration and visual research into simple or complex images that can be transformed with colour and manipulated through repeat to create a collection of patterns for printing. It will also support your development of the additional skills necessary to resolve your design brief.

3
THE DESIGN
PROCESS

INTRODUCTION

As you move through the process of visual research, you use the fundamental skills of drawing, colour and repeat to gather ideas and imagery that you can then develop more fully in order to fulfil your design brief. What you do next with your visual research is really dependent on how you want to approach the development of the project. Exploring and developing your visual research through different processes or technologies will enable you to develop your own personal response to the design brief.

The process of design development can employ a number of strategies and techniques, including the exploration of composition, scale and pattern as well as image manipulation. Print-room processes, hand-printing and digital techniques can all be used to help you in the design-development stage. Creating patterns and visualizing your design ideas in two or three dimensions, as well as exploring the relationship between pattern and fabric, are also important to design development and completion.

Below: Nigel Atkinson's fabrics demonstrate the value he places upon craft and making. His work uses both traditional and contemporary processes to create his sumptuous and luxurious textiles. They sit comfortably within both domestic and hospitality interior settings.

Previous pages:
Michael Angove plays with pattern, composition and scale in his flowing wallpaper florals.

DESIGN DEVELOPMENT

There is no specific point at which you should stop the process of visual research – experience will enable you to judge when you have done enough. Ask yourself if you have sufficient imagery and a clear sense of direction for your ideas to enable you to answer the brief. Be careful not to rush the visual research stage; if you do not have enough imagery or ideas it can lead to a repetitive design collection.

Your next steps could include investigating your drawings further through composition and scale, scanning your drawings or downloading your photographs into a CAD programme and manipulating them via digital processes, or taking your ideas into the print room. At different stages of your project you might use all three methods to enable you to explore a range of possible design ideas and solutions, depending on the requirements of the design brief and time constraints.

While you are studying printed textile design it is valuable to try all of these approaches to see which you are most drawn to, in order to begin to evaluate your skills and develop your own methodology as a designer. You may find that you are best able to achieve your design aims as a printmaker based largely in the print room, using the processes involved to develop creative solutions. Alternatively, you may see yourself as an image maker, focusing on digital image manipulation to create design solutions. It is important that you develop skills across all approaches so that you can demonstrate flexibility in both your design thinking and your execution.

The initial drawing of flowers above is used as a starting point to build a larger group of individual flowers and leaves, which is then placed upon a striped background to suggest a possible design solution.

DEVELOPING YOUR DRAWINGS

Developing your drawings is generally the next stage in the design process after visual research. It is about focusing on the information you have gathered in your visual research regarding the elements, objects, photographs and ideas that you would like to begin to develop into designs. Again, there are no hard rules about this process, but you will see that there are various approaches that could support your thinking about the development of your imagery and ideas.

Above: Taking photographs of objects can assist you later if these are used digitally or as inspiration when drawing, whether you focus on an entire object or a detailed section of it.

Above left: Consider how independent images will integrate or contrast in different combinations.

Left: Using textured materials, media or collage might help you capture subtle surface effects of the objects that you are drawing.

Below: Using different colours to emphasize lines can begin to take your eye around an image in a particular way, developing flow.

COMPOSITION AND SCALE

One way of developing your drawings is to consider composition and scale by experimenting with organization and layout. Using your drawings of several independent elements or still-life studies, you can begin to establish ideas about how to combine different objects, textures, line qualities, photographs, surface effects, etc. into a single composition. When working from a still life or looking at a landscape, it is likely that you will have already noticed some of the relationships between different objects. This is an important aspect of design: think about how the eye flows and moves around a design and also how areas of space and areas with image help create this flow and movement.

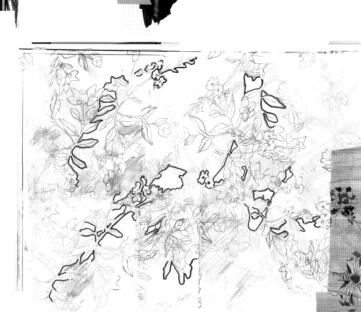

EXERCISE 1
COMPOSITION AND SCALE

◆ One way of exploring scale and composition is to photocopy five different elements or textures from your visual research at different scales, perhaps 25 per cent and 50 per cent smaller and larger, as well as in original scale (you can do this in black and white at this stage). This will give you five different scales with which you can work. Ensure that you have three or four copies of each element at each scale.

◆ Cut the individual elements out and begin to combine them or think about how you would like to use the texture, on a sheet of paper or in your sketchbook (make sure the size of the paper is appropriate in ratio to the size of your elements), mixing elements with different scales.

◆ Move them around for a while, experimenting with the relationships between how you organize the imagery, pattern and negative space. You may overlap them, or allow some of them to hang off the edges (thinking about where they might come back on the opposite side if the pattern were in repeat). There are no rules, so don't worry about your layout being exact.

◆ Allow yourself to respond visually to the images and elements, thinking about what works, and why.

Rosie Moss explores composition by photocopying her drawings at a range of different scales, enabling her to play with patterning and visual effects as she develops her design ideas.

It may be helpful to build up a collection of other art and design practitioners' work as this can inspire your approach to composition, layout and pattern. Be broad in your selection of these images as they may often come from sources such as illustration and graphics, fine art or other textile fields. You can also collect images from magazines, postcards from exhibitions and galleries or your own photographs of pattern and composition in the environment.

Top left: Artist Jen Stark uses both positive and negative space to create a sense of chaos in her energetic painted compositions.

Above: The design group Neasden Control Centre combines a range of montaged and layered imagery to create challenging compositions for its promotional designs.

Top right: Lizzie Allen creates depth in this narrative wallpaper through colour, scale and the use of negative space, as well as by layering components in varying proportions.

Right: Tilleke Schwarz uses negative space, layered with lines, marks and colour effects in various widths to create dramatic compositions.

EXERCISE 2
EXPLORING COMPOSITION THROUGH DRAWING

There are additional strategies that you can use to explore composition through drawing or redrawing your visual research. These starting points are suggestions that may help you find a direction in which to develop your visual research.

- ◆ Look at your drawing and focus upon the negative space in relation to the object or still life that you are using. Try to draw the negative space, drawing attention to the space by using colour or texture. Don't draw any detail in the object itself; allow the image to become a silhouette.

- ◆ Work on the image upside down by turning your drawings upside down and redrawing them.

- ◆ Invert or play with scale, redrawing all the elements of your image at the same size or in different proportions. You can use a mirror to help you with this by placing it in front of your drawing at an angle that creates distortions and then drawing from the distorted reflection.

- ◆ Play with scale through representing or inverting natural relationships to create a quirky and playful design – for instance, a flower could become bigger than a house.

Composition is a vital creative tool for the printed textile designer, enabling you to consider how all the elements within an image are organized, and how they influence the way in which your eye moves and flows around the design. Composition and scale help to 'interrogate' your visual research, interacting with repeat, pattern and placement to assist you in fulfilling your design brief.

Top: In Committee's playful commentary on waste, the natural proportions of the objects have been altered to suit the composition and allow the eye to flow around the design.

Above: Jane Gordon Clark explores a dramatic scale shift with this photographic floral image.

DIGITAL DESIGN DEVELOPMENT

Working with CAD opens up a range of possibilities for further development of your visual research. Drawings and paintings that you have created using traditional media can be scanned into the computer, or photographs downloaded, and these images can be manipulated using digital tools. Getting to know this software is extremely useful and there are some great guides (see 'Further Reading' on page 202) to help you develop your skills if you are not familiar with these programs.

Some designers might wish to draw directly onto the computer with a graphics tablet and digital stylus pen, rather than with a mouse, using off-the-shelf packages such as Photoshop® or Illustrator®. With a digital tablet and stylus you can also use this software to create your own bespoke motifs and images, experimenting with the range of paintbrushes on offer in Photoshop® or the graphic and linear qualities that are available in Illustrator®.

CAD programs offer a range of tools that you can use to manipulate and edit your scanned imagery, resulting in myriad design possibilities. Basic copy-and-paste tools enable you to repeat elements or motifs and, used in conjunction with basic transform tools, can allow you to change scale, flip, distort, etc. The opportunity to change and explore a range of complex colour effects is also available. Filters can be applied to distort individual motifs or whole images. Photo-manipulation allows you to produce digital montages, collages and explore photographic images in ways that were not possible in printed textile design even as recently as 20 years ago.

Some designers have also explored using the scan bed itself as a medium. By moving objects while they are being scanned you can capture movement and create images that cannot be created through manual means. Varying the timing of these movements as you scan to be quick, slow or repetitive can also create different effects.

Above: Colour changes can be implemented easily using Photoshop®, enabling you to emphasize or disguise different elements of your image.

Right: Photoshop® filters (clockwise from the top) 'blur', 'brush', 'find edges' and 'stylize' have been used to create different effects from this photograph of a fragment of lace.

Below: This image by Rachel Trenouth has been created by moving individual flowers across the scan bed as it is capturing the information, and then layering each file together.

Above left and right: Moving an item on the scan bed in different ways at regular intervals creates a regular pattern formation (left), while moving it at sporadic intervals creates a different effect (right).

Far right: This images has been digitally layered with others to create this design, which has variations of colour and texture within a structured pattern.

PRINT-ROOM PROCESSES

Designers may choose to develop their visual research through print-room processes, exploring the interrelationships between their design ideas, fabric, print processes and textural effects created through surface manipulation techniques. For some designers the printing process and the relationship between fabric and image are inspirational and lead to a strong sense of design resolution. They may be intrigued by the impact of fabric choice on the design ideas or intend to use a particular print process to enable them to add different effects to the cloth that working with paper or CAD designs cannot replicate.

Developing your design idea in the print room also involves making choices about your print process, colour palette, fabrics and dye type early in the process. There are many different methods and processes for printing images onto cloth, including stencil, transfer, relief and digital printing methods. There are also some processes that do not fit directly into any of these categories, such as monoprinting. While these may not have a direct commercial application, they can be used to support design development through their idiosyncratic visual qualities, which can then be translated into your design.

A typical studio, with fabric samples, Kodatraces, rolls of paper and useful craft and practical tools.

STENCIL PRINTING

Stencil printing describes a range of print processes that essentially use positive and negative imagery. The relationship between the positive and negative involves the use of a stencil, which can be created through a variety of means, from tearing or cutting paper to painting your design on film and exposing it photographically. The stencil maintains the positive and negative aspects of the image and therefore defines and creates boundaries where the image is being printed.

Printing onto fabric is usually carried out using a silk screen made from wood or metal onto which a fine silk mesh is stretched. The mesh enables print dyes or pigments to be pushed through it with a squeegee in an even and controlled manner. The squeegee needs to be held at an angle of around 45 degrees and pulled slowly and smoothly across the surface of the screen both forward and backwards; depending on the fabric surface, this may need to be done more than once. It is useful to have a partner to print with to enable even coverage of ink across the surface of the screen.

There are two methods you can use for silk-screen printing: paper stencils or photographic methods.

Having access to a range of screen sizes and different types of fabric will enable you to make decisions about how to develop your design ideas.

PAPER STENCILS

This process involves the creation of stenciled imagery by cutting or tearing shapes out of stable two-dimensional materials. These materials should be as thin as possible; newsprint paper is a suitable surface for this process, for example. You can also use cartridge paper or acetate sheets to create your stencils; acetate is particularly useful if you would like to reuse the stencil. The stencil can be used to print a shape or motif, or can also be used to block out areas of the print.

STEP 1
Tape your fabric or paper down to the print table and place your stencil on top. Make sure that you have the right size of squeegee for the screen that you are using.

STEP 2
Place the screen down on the fabric and begin to pour your dye along the top edge of the stencil. Try to keep the dye even and in a straight line.

STEP 3
Positioning the squeegee at a slight angle, pull the ink towards you with even pressure.

STEP 4
Lift the screen away, pulling one side up at an angle.

STEP 5
Wash the screen immediately so that the dye does not solidify on the mesh.

WHEN USING A SQUEEGEE YOU NEED TO APPLY EVEN PRESSURE AS WELL AS CREATING ENOUGH TENSION FOR IT TO GLIDE ACROSS THE SCREEN SMOOTHLY. IF YOU PRESS TOO HARD IT WILL JUDDER AND IF YOU DON'T PRESS HARD ENOUGH IT WON'T PUSH THE INK THROUGH THE MESH.

PHOTOGRAPHIC STENCILS

The production of a photographic stencil requires you to translate your drawing, photograph, or image into a format with which you can create a photo-stencil known as a 'positive'. The photo-stencil, or positive, is then transferred to the screen, which has been coated with a light-sensitive emulsion, by exposing it in a darkroom using a photochemical process.

If you are painting directly onto the film, then you need to work with a specialist product such as Kodatrace transparent tracing film, together with a special opaque fluid or Indian ink as your medium. The fluid has a consistency enabling you to paint or use other tools to apply it to the film. Alternatively, you can produce images with the aid of a photocopier or print directly from a CAD system onto your film or acetate. Whichever method you use, it is essential that the image, marks or design are opaque and do not let any light through. If they are not you may have to touch up areas with the opaque fluid. You can check for opaqueness by holding the film up to the light or placing it on a light box, ensuring that you cannot see light through it.

STEP 1

Using your original image secure it to the light box using tape. Remember that each colour in the design requires separating onto film. In this image there are nine colours but the designer is going to separate it into three colours using light, mid and dark to identify each shade.

STEP 2

You need a ruler, a set square, a black pen, transparent film and opaque black fluid as well as brushes. A chinagraph pencil may also be useful. Tape the film down on top of the image and, using a set square, draw crosshairs in the corners. This is so that you can make sure the images are in the same place on each piece of film and will help you line the images up on top of each other when you are printing them.

STEP 3

To create a separation, choose one colour and, using an appropriately sized brush, begin to paint out all of the areas on the image that are that colour. Take care to ensure that the paint is as flat as possible.

STEP 4

When you have painted out one colour tape down the next sheet of transparent film and draw the crosshairs using a ruler in each corner.

STEP 5

Identify the colour you are painting over this time and again using an appropriate size brush begin this colour separation.

STEP 6

Continue painting until all of your colours have been painted out.

STEP 7

This is an example of one of the colour separations from this series.

COLOUR SEPARATIONS

When printing with a silk screen there are many combinations and approaches that you can take to reproduce your images. You can work with simple one-colour images or you can build up layers of images and colours to create more complex designs. As you experiment with various combinations, you will develop your visual research towards the establishment of your pattern and colour palette.

Creating a multicoloured screen print requires the creation of a stencil for each colour within the design onto a separate layer, known as a colour separation or, in the case of photographic stencils, a transparency. Because this process of separating the colours can be completed by hand-painting, drawing or photography, the artist's style can be translated easily. Each separation is used to create a separate screen; the screens are then printed independently to build up the full colour image. This method is often used in industry for sampling. It is also the most common method used by textile design students in university and art school print workshops.

Top: This four-colour stylized print by Romo, available in seven different colourways, was inspired by its archive of 1930s designs.

Above: Sanderson have produced 'Eglantine' with a broad range of colours. This creates a more naturalistic floral image. 'Eglantine' is from their 'Vintage' fabric and wallpaper collection.

Below: This motif is made of two colours that we can see as separate images, which are then brought together to create the two-colour motif.

Each screen has cost implications because it affects how long the design will take to be printed and how many separations are required, as well as the production of another batch of print paste. Therefore, it is important that each colour is chosen carefully to ensure it has a purpose within the design. Such colour restrictions are sometimes thought by students to hamper creativity, but working within these parameters can inspire a more innovative approach. Many designers pride themselves on being able to make a five-colour print look like much more.

Left and below: The screens required to create this design by Victoria Robinson break down into the four individual separations below. These separations are fairly even in their colour distribution, ensuring an efficient, economic use of each screen.

Mustard yellow   Taupe   Off-white   Dark brown

FOUR-COLOUR PROCESS PRINTING

If you wish to use a photographic image or print using more than a few colours, you can develop your imagery digitally and colour separate it using CAD programs into the colours of cyan, magenta, yellow and black (CMYK). Four-colour process printing can produce excellent-quality printing and colour resolution with near-photographic accuracy, but it is a very skilled process and requires the use of extremely precise printing skills.

Each of the four colours will have its own positive, or photo-stencil, which is then transferred to a screen via a photochemical process. It is essential for accurate printing that these colour separations are completed carefully; you can check the alignment of the colour separations by placing them one on top of the other to ensure you have captured all the elements you wish to use. When the CMYK separations are layered together in the print process, the final result is seen in a full range of colours, at photographic quality if required.

Cyan   Magenta   Yellow   Black

The colour separations for this ethereal image by Rachel Trenouth have been completed by separating the image into the colours cyan, magenta, yellow and black (CMYK). The four-colour process system is useful for photographic-quality images, where separating each colour independently would be prohibitive.

RELIEF PRINTING

Relief printing describes processes in which the surface of a material, such as cork, lino, soft wood or potato, is cut or carved with your motif or image, similar to block printing.

A linocut can be printed by using a roller to apply the ink or dye to the surface of the lino, whereas a stamp, such as a potato, can be pressed directly into ink before printing. Alternatively, you can glue objects to a surface, such as thick card, which can then be dipped in ink or dye and pressed directly onto a surface of fabric and paper. This method of pressing objects into ink or dye can also be used to create a unique image by using random objects, such as the bottom of bottles or corks, feathers or leaves, or any other everyday objects you find interesting. These images and effects can then be scanned and developed further using a CAD program, enabling you to add a naive or handcrafted aesthetic to a commercially repeatable product.

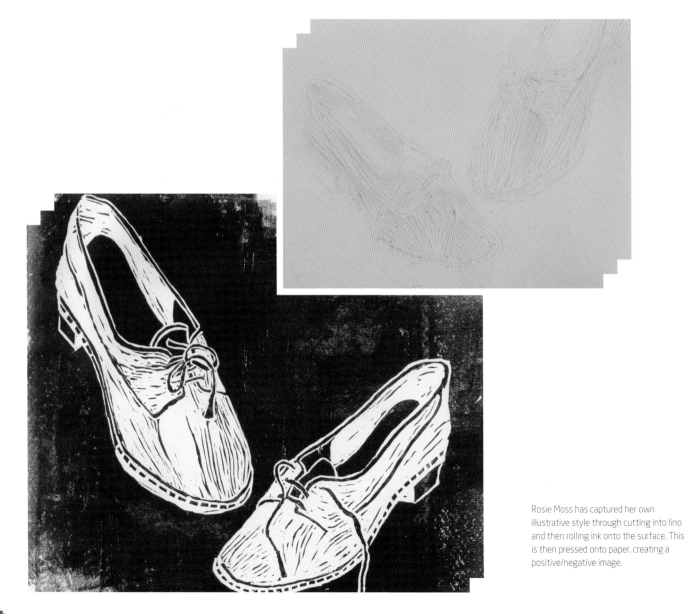

Rosie Moss has captured her own illustrative style through cutting into lino and then rolling ink onto the surface. This is then pressed onto paper, creating a positive/negative image.

TRANSFER PRINTING

Transfer printing works by using specially formulated inks that are applied to a substrate and, through the application of heat, are transferred across to another substrate. Transfer printing can be used on a variety of surfaces but works most effectively on synthetic fabrics such as polyester; prints on fabrics that are not completely synthetic will have less colour intensity.

Transfer printing is a relatively quick and easy way to develop your visual research early in the process by 'striking off' your image or design in the print studio with near-photographic accuracy. You are not required to put your design into repeat, but can transfer print small sections of fabric as you experiment with the composition, scale and colour.

Above right: Inks for transfer printing come in concentrated liquid form. To ensure that you achieve the desired colours you will need to spend time testing them.

Below and right: The textile artist Shelley Goldsmith often uses transfer printing in her work, printing onto reclaimed garments. These clothes have been printed with imagery that is suggestive of emotion and memory: the shirt is linked to flooding and seepage and the dress to human frailty.

STEP BY STEP 3
DIRECT TRANSFER PRINTING

Transfer printing onto fabric can be completed both directly and indirectly. You apply the transfer media – inks, dyes or crayons – to paper and then, through the use of heat, transfer it to fabric. You can also buy papers that you can place through digital printers to transfer CAD images or photocopied images in colour or black and white.

You may have access to a transfer press where heat and time controls can be set automatically; or you can use an iron, which may take some trial and error to time the process correctly. For future reference, make a careful note of the fabric type, the settings on the iron and how long you are ironing.

Alice Preston has used yarn to create this negative, fluid, thread-like indirect-transfer image, and has also placed pre-transfer dyed feathers on top of the thread. Combining processes can often lead to interesting results.

STEP 1
Soak or paint your chosen objects - in this example feathers - in transfer ink. Place the objects directly on top of the fabric that you wish to use.

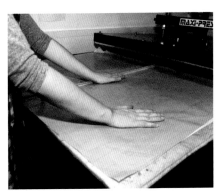

STEP 2
Cover this with some clean newsprint paper, followed by the protective sheet that should be used with the transfer press.

STEP 3
Following the time instructions for your transfer press, engage the image and the press for the specified time and stay close as it is not usually for very long.

STEP 4
Remove the protective cover and paper.

STEP 5
Here is the transferred image of the feathers on fabric.

STEP 6
In this example dipped and painted lace and feathers were used as well as a strip of transfer paper, which is available from florists.

In indirect transfer printing, objects such as lace, feathers or leaves are used to create negative images within your design. The objects will block the transfer of pattern, leaving their silhouette on the substrate in reverse.

By painting directly onto paper with transfer inks and cutting shapes out of the paper, then rearranging them, Alice Preston has created this direct-transfer-printed image with a fractured and dynamic composition.

ENSURE THAT THE
PAPER AND THE
FABRIC ONTO WHICH
YOU ARE PRINTING
ARE THE SAME SIZE

STEP 1
Paint an entire sheet of paper with transfer ink dye. Place the objects you have selected - here they are motifs cut from a piece of lace - onto the fabric on which you wish to print.

STEP 2
Place the painted piece of paper face down on top of the objects.

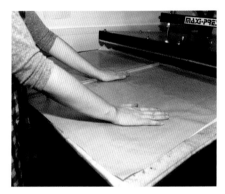

STEP 3
Place a protective sheet of paper on top of the painted piece of paper.

STEP 4
Having previously heated the press to the temperature appropriate for the fabric you are using, close the press.

STEP 5
Open the press and remove the protective piece of paper.

STEP 6
Remove the painted piece of paper.

STEP 7
Remove the objects to reveal the negative shapes left on the fabric.

STEP 8
The final printed fabric.

COLLAGRAPH PRINTING

Collagraph printing involves the creation of a three-dimensional collage by gluing and sticking objects to a cardboard backing, which you can then use to print and emboss paper using a printing press.

Glue your chosen objects to the card and apply a layer of varnish. When the varnish on the collagraph is completely dry you can then rub ink onto the surface. For printing, use watercolour paper that is soaked in water for a short while; blot away any excess water. Place the paper over the top of the inked collagraph and place in a printing press; this will have a very heavy roller through which your collagraph is passed, protected by foam padding above and below. The printing press ensures even coverage when transferring the print to the paper.

Collagraph printing can capture a range of different textures and effects, from the subtle qualities of leaves to bolder bubble wrap or string. This process has great creative potential, which can be further developed by transferring images into digital format or onto a screen print in order to explore scale and pattern-making.

STEP 1

You can use a wide range of objects or textured surfaces to create a collagraph print, however, the surface should not be raised any higher than 5mm (⅕in). Begin by gluing your objects to the card, then wait for the glue to dry.

STEP 2

When your collagraph has dried, paint the surface with clear varnish. This protects the surface so that you can use it repeatedly. Again, wait for the surface to dry.

STEP 3

Rub a relief-printing ink directly onto your collagraph. You can use a cloth to do this, using your finger to rub the ink into all the nooks and crannies to ensure that the ink is fairly even across the surface. You may need to wipe ink off as well as on.

STEP 4

Using watercolour paper for printing is advisable as it is tougher than cartridge paper; it will need to be soaked for a few minutes and then pressed between blotting paper to remove excess water.

STEP 5

Place the paper on top of the inked collagraph and place it on the printing press. Most printing presses will have blankets or sponge to protect the print from the very heavy rollers, and it is important that you ensure that your work is covered with these.

STEP 6

Roll the press evenly over your collagraph once.

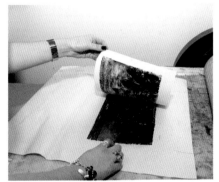

STEP 7

You can now look at your print. You may find that there is enough ink to print another image, or you may wish to produce another print with another colour. If so, clean your collagraph and repeat the process.

DIGITAL (INKJET) PRINTING

Digital printing is the term often used to describe printing directly onto fabric through an inkjet printing process, whereby images that have been created by digital means or digitized from manual methods are transferred onto fabric.

Digital printing on fabric is generally completed at a printing bureau. Colleges or universities may have their own printers that you can access, though these are likely to be operated by a member of the technical staff. This is usually due to the costs of the machine and the technical knowledge required.

Once you have developed your design, either by hand or in CAD, you will inevitably still need to consider the relationship between the colours on the screen and the colours as they are printed, keeping in mind that the colours you have chosen on screen will not be reproduced exactly the same in print unless colour-management software is used. Variations in colour calibration from one device to the next, and differences in various fabrics and substrates, will also alter your results.

In digital printing, achieving the colours you desire may be done in two ways: either by carrying out manual adjustments and colour tests or by incorporating separate colour-management software into the set-up of a digital print studio.

Once you are sure you are happy with the quality of the print and have made the correct fabric choice, you can also consider using other manual print techniques on top of your digital print, such as flock, foil, puff and devoré, to add surface texture or effects.

Above and right: Digital printing enables you to print texture, block colour and tonal gradations all in the same design. Josh Goot's signature style uses this potential in the way he approaches his bright, energetic and graphic prints.

Right: The same image is printed here on three different fabrics: linen, chiffon and cotton. The fabric and dye will affect how your colours appear.

Below: A digital print technician is setting up an image to be printed directly onto fabric.

Bottom: Printing samples of your designs and your colour palette before their final production can enable you to be confident about colour accuracy.

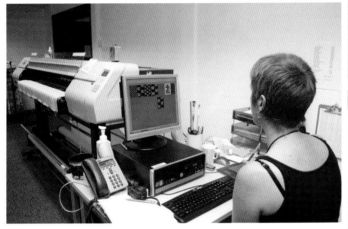

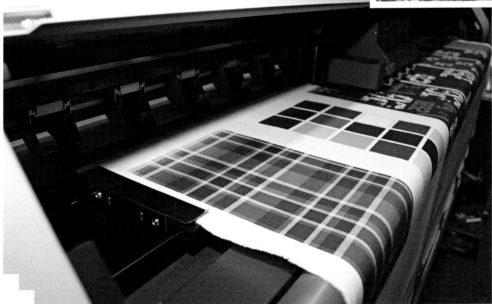

MONOPRINTING

The term monoprinting refers to a method that creates a single individual print. There are three separate processes described as monoprinting: reactive monoprinting, indirect monoprinting and direct monoprinting. These methods apply drawing and mark-making techniques to create individual monotone or multicoloured images by painting directly onto the screen with dyes, or drawing into a surface that has previously had ink applied to it.

STEP BY STEP 6
REACTIVE MONOPRINTING

Using this process you can paint directly onto a silk screen using reactive dyes to create a range of marks, textures or imagery.

To paint your design onto the screen, place an image or sketch of your design underneath your screen to use as a guide. Place the screen resting on its frame, which will leave a gap between the mesh and your design. After allowing your design to dry, flip the screen over so that the painted side is against the substrate that you wish to print on. Using a squeegee, pull a clear print paste (manutex) through the screen; this will transfer the image onto your chosen surface. This method also reproduces the texture of the screen, adding another visual quality. While it is possible to print the image more than once, it is important to note that the colour intensity will reduce with each repetition.

STEP 1

Place your screen on the table mesh-side up so that this is not touching the table. Using reactive dyes, paint directly onto the screen. You will be able to use more than one colour, but make sure that you let each one dry before applying the next - if they are wet, they will bleed.

STEP 2

When you have finished painting your design, either allow your image to air dry, or use a hair dryer (making sure you keep the dryer moving constantly).

STEP 3

Alternatively, if you have access to one, you may find it easier to use a drying cabinet.

STEP 4

When your design is completely dry, lay it mesh-side down onto paper that has been taped to the table (it is likely that you will be able to produce more than one print so you may like to prepare a couple of extra sheets of paper). Apply an even, straight line of manutex along the top of the screen.

STEP 5

Using an appropriately sized squeegee for your image and screen, and angling it slightly, pull the manutex towards you with a smooth, steady tension.

STEP 6

Lift the screen up from one side to help ensure that you are not pulling on the paper. If you wish to do another print, do so immediately, and then wash your screen.

BEAR IN MIND THAT WHEN YOU FINALLY PRINT YOUR IMAGE, IT WILL BE REVERSED.

Opposite: This design by Jo Williams is part of a collection in which all the images were hand-painted directly onto screen as a monoprint, then scanned and printed digitally. This allowed her to preserve the effects of this process in the final digital prints.

INDIRECT MONOPRINTING

This method of transferring ink onto paper or fabric requires you to apply ink, using a roller or brush, onto a flat, non-absorbent surface such as glass, acrylic or plastic. Once the surface is covered, you can use any tools to make marks into the paste such as sticks, pens, brushes or cloth; or you could make impressions with textured objects such as leaves or a sponge. Once the image is finished, place a piece of fabric on the surface and gently rub with your hand across the whole length and width of the fabric. Lift the substrate carefully and leave it to dry naturally.

STEP 1
Roller your ink paste onto a flat, smooth surface such as glass, acrylic or plastic. This should be around the same size as the substrate on which you wish to print.

STEP 2
Draw or texturize the surface with whatever tools feel appropriate for what you would like to draw. The areas where you are removing the ink from the surface will produce a negative line in your image.

STEP 3
Place a piece of paper or fabric on top of your finished design and gently and smoothly press across the surface.

STEP 4
Lift the paper or fabric carefully from the surface and allow the ink to dry. Make sure you clean the surface that you have been working on before it dries.

Opposite: Indirect monoprinting captures a negative linear image; the texture of the ink adds to the quality of the effect.

DIRECT MONOPRINTING

Direct monoprinting takes a slightly different approach, whereby the ink is applied to the printing surface in the same way but then the fabric or paper is placed directly onto this surface. You then draw directly onto the fabric, being careful not to lean on the fabric or paper while you are drawing. You can use different colours by having more than one colour rollered onto your printing surface in stripes, patterns or blocks, or you can print in stages by drying and then replacing the fabric or paper onto different coloured surfaces, enabling you to build a multicoloured image.

These three methods of monoprinting create marks, line qualities and textures that are intrinsic to the process and can be developed to give a spontaneous feel to your images. Indirect and direct monoprinting give a quality of line that is crisp but the edges are also softened with texture, and they create textural interplay between the ink and the print substrate. Your monoprinted images can then be scanned into the computer and be further developed digitally into patterns and resolved designs.

Top: Direct monoprints recreate the spontaneous, linear feel of hand-drawing but with softened lines and a textural quality. Emma Moloney uses the technique in illustrations, often in combination with other media.

Above and left: Martina Paukova used the monoprinting process to draw a group of individual gates, which she then scanned and used to create patterns.

STEP 1
Roller your ink paste onto a flat, smooth surface such as glass, acrylic or plastic. This should be around the same size as the substrate on which you wish to print.

STEP 2
Place the paper or fabric on top of the rollered ink gently, being careful not to press on it too hard.

STEP 3
Draw onto the paper with a mark-making tool – you need to put enough pressure on the paper to ensure it picks up the ink from the surface below.

STEP 4
When you have finished, lift your design and let it dry. Make sure you clean the surface that you have been working on before it dries. Notice that in this type of print you have a positive linear image.

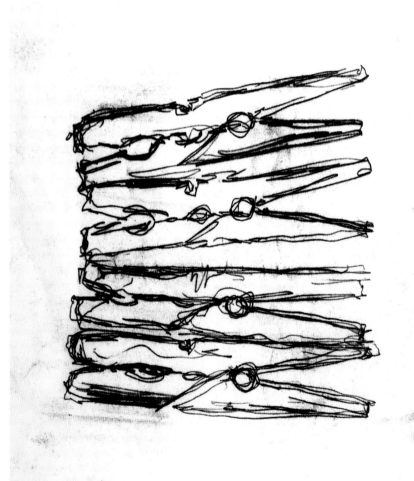

SURFACE MANIPULATION

Both screen and digital printing open up the possibility of using additional processes to create fabrics that have surface texture or dimensional effects. These processes alter the surface qualities of the fabric by introducing effects such as puff binder, flocking or foil, or by extracting fibres or colour from the surface of the fabric through devoré, discharge or illuminating-discharge printing. The surface effects are created by the combination and application of chemicals to the dyestuffs being used.

The heat press is a useful tool for achieving interesting printing effects such as flocking or foiling, in which specialized fabric glue is screen-printed or painted onto fabric and heat is applied to adhere the foil to the area. Screen-print your image with an adhesive directly onto the fabric, then lay the sheet of foil or flock on top of the glued area. Cover with a top layer of fabric or paper to provide some protection, and, using a heated iron, apply enough pressure to adhere the foil or flock to the fabric.

Puff binder is created by mixing an expanding chemical into ink for pigment printing, and then printing as normal. The binder then requires baking to cure the expanding puff pigment. It is also possible to create shimmering images by mixing metallic binders or powders into printing pigments.

Devoré printing, also known as 'burn-out' printing, uses a print paste containing a strong acid that will destroy or burn out any areas of natural or cellulosic fibre in a fabric woven from a combination of cellulosic and synthetic fibres. The synthetic fibres will be left intact, with the printed pattern appearing as sheer areas within the fabric. This technique is quite old and some of the chemicals used can be dangerous or polluting, and may be regulated by law or even prohibited in some areas.

Discharge and illuminating-discharge printing involve printing with a discharge agent to remove or replace colour from a fabric that has first been either dyed or printed with dischargeable dye. When the discharge agent is applied, it creates a pattern by removing the colour with which it has come into contact. In the case of illuminating-discharge printing, the paste contains a dye that replaces the ground colour with a second colour. Discharge prints are expensive to produce, but are prized due to the depth of colour and print detail achieved on both sides of the fabric.

The raised surface of flock creates interesting surface effects, as in this fabric by Suzanne Goodwin. She has added another dimension by including a chemical that reacts to ultraviolet (UV) light. Here are two images of the same fabric, one taken in daylight and one in UV light.

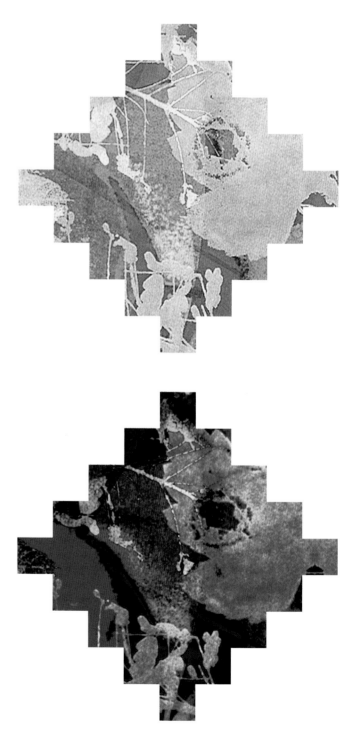

Left: This design, 'Cameo', is by English Eccentrics designer Helen David, who is well known for her sophisticated use of devoré, which burns out the cellulosic fibres from mixed-fibre fabrics.

Below: This wallpaper by Georgie Worker has been created using a specialized adhesive on which foils can be applied using a heat press or iron. She has used this process in her wallpaper collection to explore matt and shiny effects.

Bottom: Discharge printing uses a chemical to remove or replace dischargeable dye from areas of a previously dyed or printed fabric. Dawn Dupree uses this technique in her printing to create a textural effect.

MOVING TOWARDS A FINISHED DESIGN

While you are exploring the various methods of developing your design you should be in the process of reflecting and evaluating what works effectively, what does not, and why. Your ability to make the decisions necessary to complete your project depends on this evaluation. You should also share your work with your colleagues to benefit from their advice and opinions; design tutorials should enable you to gather your peer group's view and help develop your own judgement. Try to ensure that you fully explore the different suggestions that other people make; evaluate them visually, as opposed to just in your head. At this point in the process you should also re-examine your design brief and ensure that you are meeting its requirements.

You will be developing a range of strategies that help you to answer the brief fully. These include pattern or placement, the relationship of your design to the product and the fabric choices you are making, always keeping in mind the requirements of your brief, including the target market for your designs.

These three images show how Natalie Dawson is trying to develop her design ideas by thinking about the trompe l'œil effects of folded paper and origami design.

PATTERN AND PLACEMENT

Pattern and repeat can be considered similar in that they both produce designs that include qualities of repetition and structure. But they differ in that pattern relates essentially to the imagery and its visual and aesthetic effects, while repeat is a technical function: the ability to print something in a cohesive way across the width and length of a fabric. While elements of repeat may be evident in a pattern, some patterns are not put into repeat at all but might be used as placements, engineered prints or non-repeating digital fabric prints.

If you use a single motif to create a pattern, for example, the repetition (or lack of it) is a powerful aspect of the pattern. Alternatively, if your design uses several different visual elements along with devices such as scale, media, colour and texture, then the power of the image lies in the interplay of the different components. It is useful, therefore, to think about whether your pattern will be simple or complex, static or flowing and rhythmical.

Successful commercial work uses pattern being in a variety of ways. Orla Kiely, for instance, is a leader in contemporary printed textiles and has made pattern her trademark. Her approach is very simple and effective, often using a motif with a simple block or half-drop repeat.

Left: A simple motif used with a limited colour palette can create dramatic variation. In this design by Nisha Crossland, she has employed a simple linear flower, organized in an organic and multidirectional format.

Below right: Miu Miu combines a strong repeat with varied line qualities and the use of positive and negative space to keep the eye moving in this highly structured design.

Below left: In this structured half-drop design from Orla Kiely, a simple and crisp floral is enhanced by rotation and tonal gradation.

A more complex approach to pattern can be found in the work of significant textile designers such as William Morris (1834–96) and Lucienne Day (1917–2010). Morris, a founder of the Arts and Crafts movement, focused upon organic and natural forms. Morris' designs use repeat in a highly repetitive manner but his skilled approach resulted in designs that appear flowing and organic, as though branches and flowers are undulating and growing in front of you.

Day explored the relationship between art and science with her designs and was also inspired by the abstract artists Paul Klee and Jean Miró, incorporating spatial organization and the relationship between negative and positive space to create flow and balance in her designs.

The fact that these designers' work is still being sold decades after being created is testament to their exceptional skill and the impact of their patterns. The scale, colour and product applications of their designs might change (Morris' prints have been applied to everything from handkerchiefs to greetings cards), but the enduring qualities of the patterns do not.

Top and above: Lucienne Day designed 'Calyx' in 1954 (top) – the half-drop is quite hard to spot due to the complexity of lines and shapes used. It is now available to buy as a digital print in a range of colourways (above).

Left: 'Strawberry Thief' by William Morris uses a highly structured mirror repeat, but with complex, multilayered organic shapes and undulating structures.

Far left: Half-drop repeats tend to give a more organic effect than a block repeat – this is 'Hollis', by Surfacephilia.

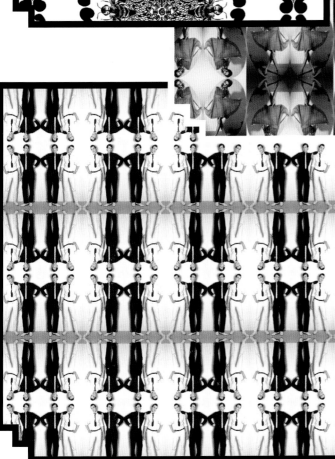

Left: With her signature black-and-white imagery, Johanna Basford uses a classic ogee pattern to create a rhythmic vertical flow. The fine details of the linear drawing are enhanced by contrasting areas of solid black.

Below and bottom left: Rachel de Joode develops images from art, photography and fashion using mirror and turnover repeats in order to create her kaleidoscope wallpapers.

Bottom right: Basso & Brooke use mirror imagery to create a dramatic symmetry in this coat from the company's autumn/winter 2009 collection.

NON-REPEATING PATTERN

The development of CAD programs and digital printing has made it possible to create and print non-repeating patterns, which may seem to be a contradiction in terms. Several research projects have been developed that consider how to generate and randomize non-repeating pattern. The non-repeating pattern can be generated and then digitally printed at any desired length and scale, limited only by the computer's ability to deal with the file size.

Right: Hilary Carlisle has developed software that allows a range of parameters to be altered, controlling how a motif or line continues along the length and breadth of a fabric. In these two fabrics the movement, width and colour of lines were altered. The pattern can be digitally printed and generated continuously, with no repetition.

Above: Devabrata Paramanik has worked with new methods of image capture that can lead to continuous pattern generation. These three patterns were generated by using webcams to record movement.

ENGINEERED PRINTS AND PLACEMENTS

Textile and graphic designers are often involved in developing design ideas for T-shirts where a single pattern or motif is placed to create a particular effect. A placement print is a design that may be applied to the garment in exactly the same place each time. Unlike most textile printing, this type of print is usually applied to a finished T-shirt or garment.

In engineered prints there is a strong relationship between the pattern and the design of the product or garment. The print may be designed so that a particular motif or design element will always fall on the garment in the same place; for example, around the neckline or across the chest. Prints are often engineered so that they appear to work 'seamlessly' around the body, taking into consideration how the garment is to be cut and sewn.

This is in contrast to the general approach, whereby each component of the garment is cut as efficiently as possible, from the same length of fabric with little consideration of how joins might emerge. If you intend to develop your designs as engineered patterns, you will need to develop methods by which to interpret and test your two-dimensional ideas in three dimensions so that you can assess these inter-relationships.

Fashion designer Holly Fulton uses engineered placement prints to make a strong statement on her simple silhouettes.

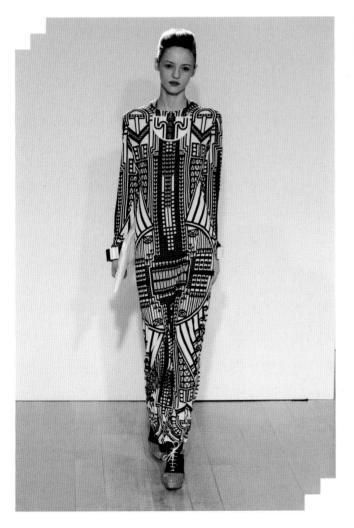

WORKING FROM TWO TO THREE DIMENSIONS AND VISUALIZATION

If you wish to develop your ideas for engineered prints, or you are contemplating a design decision regarding product application processes, then there is a range of strategies that you can use to refine your thinking or test your designs. These methods will help you to consider the relationship between the scale of the design and the finished product, how the print will work across seams or around the form of the product, or compositional factors and how images might interact with the body or object. They include working between two and three dimensions, creating a toile, projecting your designs onto a garment or creating a visualization of alternative design applications.

When working directly on a garment stand, you can begin to see the impact of the placement of particular details on the fabric's overall form on the body, going from two to three dimensions. In this instance a small section of fabric was pleated and its placement on the neck and shoulders explored. Taking photographs as you drape will enable you to evaluate and reflect on your work.

Right and below: The application of textiles to different types of product brings different design challenges. This concept-car digital visualization enabled Mary Crisp to explore the scale, placement and form of her designs for car seating.

Bottom left and right: By projecting several different versions of her design and removing excess visual information, Sarah Patterson was able to group her ideas for further reflection.

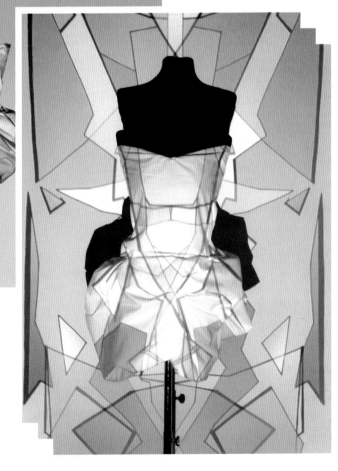

FABRIC

As discussed earlier in the chapter, most designers tend to work predominately with either images or print processes to develop their design ideas into a print collection. If you are working through print processes then it is important that you are aware of the relationship between print and fabric, and that the choice of fabric will affect the look of the print. No matter which design or printing strategy you prefer, it is important that you consider the fabric choices appropriate to the function of the product as described in your design brief. Floaty and feminine dresses might be made of chiffon or silk organza, while upholstery fabrics need to be hard-wearing and, therefore, might be made of heavy cotton. Alternatively, you may wish to invert or challenge conventions by using fabric in an inverse way to its most appropriate use, such as printing on upholstery fabric for a fashion product, thus creating innovative and quirky outcomes.

You should also be aware of the cost of the fabric you choose for your collection and ensure that it is suitable for the market level specified in your design brief. Spend some time researching the fibre content, fabric weight and construction of a range of garments and household textiles at various market levels in order to understand this relationship. You can compare and evaluate fabrics by checking the websites of fabric manufacturers or by looking at the fabrics stocked within digital print bureaux.

Above right: Buying the fabric that you wish to use can be time-consuming, but websites such as this one from Whaleys can be a very useful resource.

Right: Different levels of the market will use different fabrics and fibres. This dress by Emma Cook is targeted towards the high end of the market; it is made from silk, which is considered exclusive and is expensive. A garment made for the lower end of the market might pick up on a similar trend, in this case animal print, but may be made from a fabric of lesser quality.

MOVING ON

The process of design development moves the print designer from initial visual research through a variety of methods, strategies and decision-making processes that will allow a design idea or visual image to evolve towards a print collection and the fulfilment of the design brief. As you develop your ideas, you are learning and practising an array of techniques, from composition and scale, digital manipulation and print-room processes to an understanding of pattern, placement and fabric options. At the same time, you are learning about yourself as a print designer: your style, skills, preferences and shortcomings. Armed with this body of knowledge and technical proficiency, you are ready to explore the real world of textile manufacturing and printing with its various manufacturing methods and issues that will influence your designs.

Above: 009 Textiles' design style is bold and dramatic – in this instance the studio uses recognizable imagery, engineering the print to create this statement armchair.

Left: The design duo Draw In Light produces unique garments in which the print and garment shape enhance each other.

4
MANUFACTURING, MATERIALS AND DESIGN CHOICES

INTRODUCTION

As you progress in acquiring the skills, knowledge and abilities needed to practise as a printed textile designer, it is also important that you develop an understanding of how textiles are manufactured, and of your role as a designer in relation to manufacturing methods and its position in the supply chain. Your involvement with the process of manufacture will differ depending on where you work in the industry, whether you are working independently as a designer, consulting with a brand or retailer, or employed by a textile company.

There are many questions to be asked, and decisions to be made, in the journey that a textile design goes through on its way to becoming a printed fabric or a manufactured product. These include choosing raw materials, printing methods and finishes. Understanding how various manufacturing processes affect the choices you must make as a designer will enable you to stretch the boundaries of what is possible in order to create innovative and exciting textile products.

An increasingly important consideration in the design, manufacture and life cycle of a textile product is the issue of sustainability and design responsibility. Textiles are resource-intensive products, from raw materials through their manufacturing processes, transportation, wear and care and disposal. Companies involved throughout the supply chain are now taking issues of design responsibility more seriously, and today's designers need to be aware of sustainability issues to enable them to explore alternative approaches to producing textile designs.

Previous spread: Simon Cook produces striking designs for editorial illustrations, logos and fashion. This 'Boffin' Stone and Spear vs. Lucy Jay silk handkerchief combines photographic imagery with whimsical graphics.

Below: Printed textile designers working in the Colorfield Design Studio produce around ten designs per week, which are sold to fashion-forward companies from Kenzo to K-Mart.

THE DESIGNER'S RELATIONSHIP WITH MANUFACTURING

Your role as a designer and your impact on the overall decision-making in relation to how the fabric and eventual product are made will depend upon your place within the manufacturing and supply chain. In the textile industry the design and manufacturing operations can work in isolation from each other, or can be closely connected. As a self-employed freelance designer you may sell your designs via an agent, which means you will have no contact with the process or the purchaser; a designer working for a studio may be involved in overseeing the manufacture and subsequent product application; and a designer–maker is likely to be involved directly with producing and selling his or her own textiles and products.

Your relationship with production may also be determined partly by the size of company you work for: large companies tend to have departments that deal with the different aspects of the supply chain, while smaller companies might expect a more flexible approach from a few employees involved with a whole range of activities.

Manufacturing of textiles requires you to meet commercial technical parameters, such as repeat or number of colours in a design, and to ensure that the process is efficient and takes account of costs. It is also important, however, that at the more innovative and creative ends of the market designers and print manufacturers engage with designing in a way that challenges the potential of the print process, with a view to developing both printing capabilities and aesthetics.

At Standfast & Barracks, fabrics are printed using rotary screen printing – the fastest and most widely used method of print production. Each screen prints a separate colour in the design.

TEXTILE MANUFACTURING METHODS

Textile design is heavily influenced by methods of manufacture. There are many choices a designer can make, from the pattern and repeat to the number of colours to types of finishes, all interrelated with the printing process and manufacturing methods employed.

The design, manufacture and sales of printed textiles take place in all regions of the world but primarily in Asia, where manufacturers in China, India and Turkey are now mainly responsible for bulk production. When a design is going to be manufactured, it is very likely that it will be sent, generally as digital information, to another part of the world. The choice of a manufacturer for bulk production will depend on the combination of expertise, price and quality at a particular textile mill. Global communication, either virtually or in person, is commonplace in the textile design industry and designers often have to travel to oversee print production.

In general there are three main decisions to be made in relation to printing a design for any type of textile product: the substrate, or type of fabric; the appropriate dyestuff; and the printing method. The choice of fabric type, along with design qualities, market level, costs and performance requirements, will influence the printing process and dyestuffs to be used. These choices will be affected by the style, function, performance characteristics, cost and market level of the end product, and may in turn influence the region and factory chosen for production.

Most bulk fabric production now takes place in highly automated Asian factories. Fabrics are generally dyed in large tanks, vats or 'jets'.

FABRIC

Your choice of fabric is highly significant to the final product because the relationship between your design and the surface quality of the fabric needs to be appropriate to both its function as well as its aesthetic requirements. Simple economics will also influence this decision, although there are many different varieties of fabric available that should enable you to choose an appropriate fabric construction and fibre type for your design and product.

The structure, surface texture and weight of a fabric should be considered when developing your print design. Most printed fabrics are either woven or knitted; and while knits tend to stretch and offer less stability than woven fabrics, a loosely woven substrate or one woven with stretch yarns may also provide some challenges in the printing process. A sheer, dimensional or hairy surface or pile fabric will also react quite differently to various printing processes; this knowledge can be used to create interesting effects.

Fabrics may be woven or knitted from yarn made of a single fibre, whether natural or synthetic; but a significant number of the fabrics that we use are made from mixes of two or more fibres. Combinations of fibres are often used to improve durability, comfort, cost or ease of care for the product. If you are using a fabric made of multiple fibre types, it is important that you can identify them and understand their qualities, as each may respond in a different way to the dyestuffs, fixatives and chemicals used in the print process.

If the print process and dyestuffs are not appropriate to the fabric and fibre then you may find the printing is uneven, or in some places may not adhere at all. For example, the dyestuffs used in heat-transfer printing are designed to work on synthetics such as polyester, and will not print correctly on fabrics made from natural fibres. Fibre mixes are vital to some speciality print processes, such as devoré, where the chemical burns away the cellulosic fibres (cotton, rayon, etc.) and leaves the other fibres intact.

Textiles, by their very nature, begin their life as a raw material. This might be as a natural plant-based fibre such as cotton, or an animal-based fibre such as wool, a petroleum-based synthetic fibre or a man-made fibre regenerated from natural materials such as cellulose. Each fabric type raises myriad ethical issues on its journey from raw material to yarn and on to product. These include issues such as water consumption, the use of non-renewable resources, the carbon footprint and the use of chemicals and pollutants.

Table: A guide to types of fibre.

NATURAL Plant-based cellulosic or 'bast' fibres	NATURAL Animal-based protein fibres	MANUFACTURED Cellulosic regenerated or derived fibres	MANUFACTURED Synthetic petroleum-based fibres	OTHERS
cotton	silk	viscose rayon	nylon	glass
hemp	wool	lycocell	acrylic	metal
jute linen		bamboo acetate	polyester polymers	

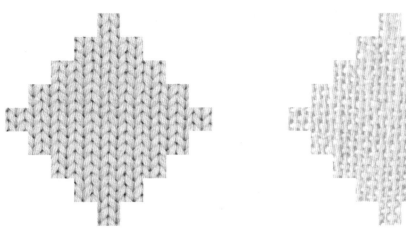

Right: Most fabrics are either knitted or woven; the process that has been used can be identified by the structures that are created. Circular or weft-knitted fabrics show a characteristic 'V' shape, while woven fabrics can be identified by their grid-like structure. Warp knits have a linear zigzag structure that can be very subtle.

COTTON

Cotton is a widely used fibre that is familiar to most consumers and is a popular and affordable choice as a fabric for printing. It can be woven or knitted into a vast array of fabric types with many different surface qualities, including textured fabrics such as towelling or cord, semi-transparent fabrics such as voile, fabrics with shine and reflection such as chintz or sateen, simply structured fabrics such as calico or cheesecloth and utility fabrics such as denim. Cotton fabrics can be lightweight or heavy, opaque or transparent, stiff or fluid, and are used for home furnishings as well as for apparel.

Cotton can be blended with other fibres such as polyester, viscose or elastane to create fabrics that may be easier to care for, better-wearing or more comfortable. Fabrics made of cotton are most often printed using pigments; as such they are moderately priced and suitable for everyday wear. Higher-end cotton fabrics may also use reactive or vat dyes and may be printed through rotary screen or digital inkjet processes for designs requiring full coverage and saturated colours.

Most of the world's cotton is grown in China, India, the USA and Pakistan. Its sustainable credentials vary widely from one area of the world to another and from one batch to another depending on its route from raw material to retail. As a crop, cotton is extremely thirsty and requires a large amount of pesticides and fertilizers, which can harm the farmer as well as pollute the water supply. Cotton can be grown organically and is seeing good success in products marketed by major brands as 'environmentally friendly', but the organic version still requires intensive irrigation.

Cotton is vulnerable to weather conditions and in recent years the crop has been severely affected by drought and floods, resulting in hoarding and speculation on the part of the world's cotton traders and an unprecedented rise in the cost of the fibre. Farmers are also turning to growing food and bio-fuel crops that offer a better profit. The use of genetically modified cotton, requiring less water and/or chemicals, has improved yields but is a subject of environmental debate.

Cotton is a cellulosic fibre, grown on plants. This series of images shows stages from field to fabric. The plants are cultivated and harvested, then taken for further processing called ginning, followed by spinning into yarn. Cotton can be woven or knitted in a wide range of structures and weights.

Above left: This design, 'Dandelion', by Angie Lewin of St Jude's, is printed on heavyweight cotton, which is easy to care for and takes colour well.

WOOL

Wool and silk account for a smaller share of the printed fabric industry and have a relatively high cost, but due to their luxurious qualities they capture our attention. The finest wool comes from Australia and New Zealand, although recently there have been campaigns in other countries for the use of local wools.

Wool is spun from the renewable fleece of animals such as sheep and goats, and some farms take steps to raise their animals organically. The practice of mulesing (cutting away skin to prevent flystrike) by many sheep farmers has been widely condemned by animal rights activists.

Wool can be made into lightweight, fluid, fine-gauge jerseys on circular knitting machines; sweater knits can be made on flatbed or fully fashioned machines, or can be woven in more traditional, hard-wearing outerwear fabrics. Wool is popular for high-end upholstery and contract fabrics for businesses, too, as it may be blended with other fibres, adding softness or strength.

Wool requires printing with acid dyes and must be bleached before processing, as it is not naturally white. Unless it is chemically treated or pre-shrunk, wool will shrink and felt when washed or steamed after printing. There are sustainable alternatives to the chlorine bleach often used to whiten and preshrink wool fibre and fabric.

However, some knitted wool fabrics may be difficult to print because the inherent characteristics of the knit mean that the fabric is not stable and the print may distort when the fabric is stretched. If the knit structure is highly textured it may also present difficulties for the dye to penetrate the fabric fully.

Above: Wool is a natural protein fibre and is sheared directly from animals such as sheep and goats. After being cleaned to remove any dirt or insects, it is classified and baled to be sent to spinners. The classification is made in microns, defined as fine, medium, fine cross-bred and coarse cross-bred. The spinners complete the scouring, carding, drawing and spinning before the wool is ready to be sent for weaving or knitting.

Left: This fabric design for Liberty, called 'Jasmine's Poppy', is printed on 100 per cent wool.

SILK

Silk offers a luxurious surface for printing and takes colour beautifully using acid or reactive dyes. The variety of silk fabrics includes a broad range of weights and drapes, from heavy and luxurious velvet to floaty and translucent chiffon. While silk does not wear with great longevity, it is often chosen for couture, high-end brands and speciality fabrics. Silk fibre can also be spun into yarn with cotton, wool, viscose, or luxury fibres such as cashmere.

Silk is sourced from silkworms, usually raised on a silk farm. The worms feed on mulberry leaves and eventually spin a silk cocoon from protein secreted by their salivary glands. The silk is extracted by boiling the cocoons and killing the pupae, which many consider to be an unethical practice. Silk is produced primarily in China and India, as well as in Europe – particularly in Italy, France and Spain.

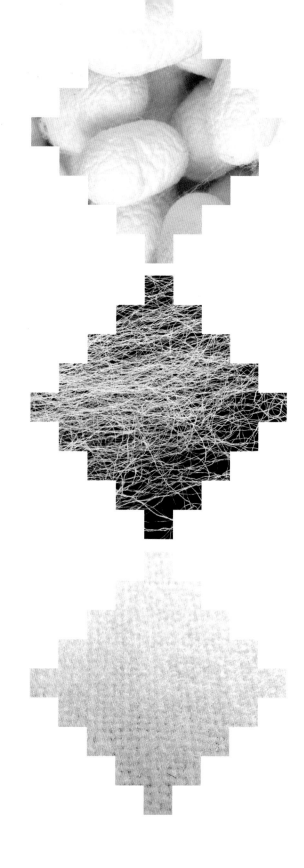

Left: A printed silk dress by Helmut Lang, made of 90 per cent silk and 10 per cent elastane – a synthetic fibre that provides stretch.

Above: Silkworms spin cocoons from a protein secreted by their salivary glands. The cocoons are collected and processed, which involves maceration, reeling, throwing the threads and degumming. Silk fibre is then spun into yarn, which can be used for weaving or knitting.

LINEN

Linen has unique qualities in terms of the range of weights and drapes available for use in the home and for fashion. Because it is stronger and less elastic than cotton it has a long association with domestic products, in particular napkins, tablecloths and tea towels. In clothing, linen is particularly prevalent in warmer seasons as it is highly absorbent and feels cool to the touch, but until recently spinners have been unable to create the really fine yarns required for lightweight, fluid fabrics and knits. However, by controlling growing and processing conditions and blending fibres, European linen spinners are now offering very fine, high thread-count products appropriate for year-round fashion fabrics. Linen prints particularly well using reactive dyestuffs or pigments.

Linen is derived from the outer 'bast' fibres of the flax plant, and is processed as a fibre mostly in northern Europe, although flax crops are grown widely in Canada, China and the USA as well. Flax gets high marks for sustainability as it is grown using crop rotation and requires little in the way of irrigation, fertilizers or pesticides. Flax is processed using an age-old, natural technique called 'retting', which involves soaking the stalks in water to separate the fibres from the core. Linen fabrics are considered sustainable as they are highly durable, making them appropriate for articles that can be used and loved for a long time.

Left: This fabric by Louise Body is digitally printed on a base that is 88 per cent linen and 12 per cent nylon. The small percentage of nylon imparts drape and makes the fabric less likely to wrinkle.

Above: Linen is a bast fibre that is sourced from flax; the plants are retted in the fields, and the fibres removed in a process known as 'scutching'.

SYNTHETIC FABRICS

There are many manufactured synthetic fibres that can be woven or knitted into fabrics, or that can be combined in yarns of various percentages with natural or cellulosic fibres. Synthetic fabrics are used in a variety of markets, particularly for sportswear, where elastane is used to provide stretch. Nylon, which was first produced in 1935, was the first synthetic fibre; a range of other synthetic fibres then appeared in the following decades, such as polyester and acrylics. Synthetic fabric responds favourably to transfer printing and can offer bright and intense colours when the correct dyestuffs are used, such as disperse and cationic dyes for polyester, and disperse or acid dyes for nylon.

There are many issues of concern about the sustainable production of synthetic fabrics from non-renewable resources such as oil, including polyester, nylon, acrylic and elastane. Some argue that their use can be sustained if the full lifetime and care of the fabric is considered and if this can be built into the design of the product.

Developments in recycled/regenerated polymers and in bio-polymers have also been explored in relation to synthetic fabrics. These bio-based polymers include Sorona®, Biophyl™ and Ingeo™, which are partially or wholly derived from corn sugars. The resulting fibres can be made into yarn and developed into fabrics for either fashion or interior uses. There has also been some development with fibres derived from milk or soy proteins in a similar fashion.

Recycled or regenerated polymers are another sustainable alternative. Plastic bottles and industrial polyester textile waste can be processed and returned to a state whereby they can be extruded as fibre and made into yarn to make fabric. Patagonia, the outdoor wear company, produces all of its polyester fleece fabric using this method. Recycled nylon yarns are developed from old fishing nets and nylon carpet scraps. Even cotton and wool fibres are being recovered from old garments and reprocessed to make new fabrics. While these recycled and regenerated fabrics present some challenges in terms of matching and dyeing colour, particularly for whites, light shades or true black, in finished products they are, for the most part, indistinguishable from new fabrics.

Above right: An electron micrograph (SEM) of polyester fibres. Polyester is a petroleum-based synthetic fibre that is extruded through spinnerets, then drawn or textured to create yarn.

Right: Ingeo™ and other bio-based synthetic fibres sourced from corn sugars can be used in a wide range of fabric structures.

Right: The Pixelkaledo poncho by Danish designer Maxjenny Forslund is printed on fabric made from 100 per cent recycled polyethylene terephthalate (PET) fibre, which is most commonly sourced from drinks bottles.

A 'pac-a-mac' from Hussein Chalayan's 'Urban Mobility' collection for Puma is printed on 100 per cent polyester, a material often chosen for sportswear.

MAN-MADE CELLULOSICS

The earliest man-made fibre was viscose rayon, which, due to its high sheen, was known as 'art silk' or artificial silk and was first commercialized by the UK company Courtaulds in 1905. The fibre was processed from wood pulp and leaves from fast-growing trees, which today are farmed and managed by the fibre producers and considered to be a renewable source. The pulp and leaves are initially dissolved in a solvent and turned into a viscous liquid that is then extruded and spun into a fibre. Unfortunately, the solvent is a pollutant and needs to be disposed of with care; in the USA the production of viscose rayon was discontinued in the 1980s due to extreme water pollution.

Viscose rayon is soft, absorbent and drapes well, but is not particularly strong when wet. High wet-modulus rayon (HWM), known as Modal, has now become the rayon of choice for many manufacturers as it is strong and durable. Bamboo rayon, processed from bamboo that grows rapidly and with little cultivation, has gained favour as a sustainable fabric in recent years, although its manufacture uses the same solvent-based process as viscose.

More recently the development of lyocell (trade name Tencel®) was established and was awarded the EU eco-label as the renewable wood pulp is dissolved in an organic petro-chemical solvent in a closed-loop manufacturing system. As a fabric it is soft, strong and drapes beautifully. Rayon and lyocell fabrics are ideal as print grounds; they take colour well and absorb reactive dyestuffs with greater intensity than cotton.

Acetate fibre is also manufactured from cellulose using a different system and chemical solvents. It takes vibrant colours using disperse dyestuffs but is generally not washable or hard-wearing; it is used primarily as a silk substitute in linings and inexpensive occasion dresses. All of the cellulosics are considered biodegradable.

Draw in Light's production methods ensure that each one of their prints is unique. This garment, '2nd Date Dress Art N Black,' is hand-screen-printed on 100 per cent viscose.

DYES AND PIGMENTS

Before the development of synthetic dyes in the mid-nineteenth century, all dyed and printed fabrics were produced using dyestuffs derived from natural sources such as berries, flowers and minerals; colours had a certain muted quality and were not fast. The first synthetic dye, called Perkin's Mauve, was produced in 1856, creating a new industry for synthetic dye manufacture and transforming the use of repeatable and reliable colour in fashion and interior textiles.

The same dyes that can be used to dye a whole length of fabric can also be used for printing, but to do this the dye needs to be turned into a paste because it needs a thicker viscosity in order to be pushed through a screen. There is a broad range of dyes that will enable you to apply colour to fabric, ranging from reactive, acid and disperse dyes to pigment inks. The choice of dye or pigment to use depends on its suitability for the fabric, for your designs and for the final product.

Several features of the dyeing process are considered damaging to the environment, in particular the chemical make-up of dyes – especially if allowed to pollute the environment when disposed of – and also the use of water for fixing. The application of colour to fabric requires certain chemicals and processes to fix the colour permanently, which is usually completed by the application of steam to the fabric. Each dyestuff has pros and cons relating to sustainability; for example, disperse dyes require high heat and pressure when used on polyester, while reactive dyes use less water than other dyes but require the use of urea to support fixing during steaming.

Mordants are required to fix dyes permanently to fabric. Among those commonly used have been metals and salts such as tannic acid, alum, urine, sodium chloride, aluminium, copper, iron, iodine and tin. There has been concern about the use of such metals as they can have a detrimental impact on those working with them, as well as on the water system if they are not treated before disposal. Using metal-free mordants or azo-free dyes (free of toxic, non-biodegradable, nitrogen-based compounds) as colourants are options printers can choose to lessen environmental impacts of dyeing and printing. The use of azos in dyeing is now banned in the European Union.

Above right: A hand-coloured copper-plate engraving of a botanical illustration of the pink-flowered indigo plant – an early source of natural indigo dyestuffs.

Right: The original sample of 'mauveine' dye, discovered by William Henry Perkin in 1856.

Working with pigments and dyes demands that health and safety guidelines are followed. It is important that you measure and mix dyes in carefully monitored and controlled environments.

When mixing pigments and dyes it can be useful to keep a technical diary or file as below to ensure that you can repeat the process in exactly the same way on another occasion. It is sensible to keep your records under the same, consistent headings so that you can make comparisons, enabling you to develop your understanding of the processes and the approaches that you can take.

DIARY HEADING	NOTES
Printing technique	Pigment, dyes or any special ingredients
Fabric	Type of fibre, where you bought it, how much it costs per metre
Fix	The type of fixing method that is required for this pigment or dye
Recipe	Details of how to prepare for printing and the ingredients and quantities that you have used
Process	Details of how to print and process the fabric; time and temperatures and number of pulls over the screen would be useful information here
Other comments	Any other comments that you have on the process, the tactile qualities of the finished fabric, things you found tricky
Sample	A small fabric sample is useful to aid your memory when you return to the process

Table: Suggested headings and contents for a technical diary to be kept when mixing pigments and dyes.

Below: The dye industry demonstrates colour ranges on shade cards or in yarn samples, as in this example from 1910.

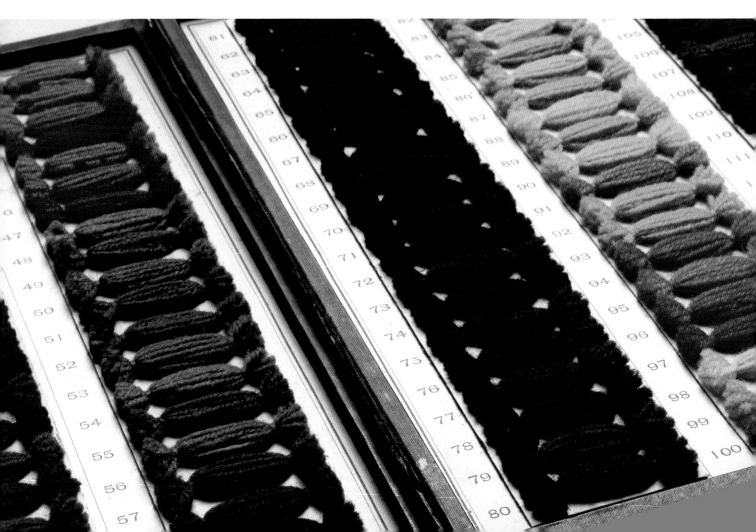

PIGMENTS

Pigments are not strictly dyestuffs because they sit on the surface of the fabric rather than being absorbed into the cloth, but as a colourant they can be applied to all types of fabric. This is the most commonly used printing technique and is used for around half of all printed textiles. Pigments are easy to mix and apply, and are relatively less expensive than printing with dyestuffs.

Pigment colours are mixed with a chemical binder or resin to adhere them to the fabric, and offer clean, sharp colours that hold their own on a dyed ground. Special binders can be added to create effects such as puff, heat-sensitive colour, metallic or pearlescent surfaces. The fabric then needs to be cured or baked at high temperatures to fix the colour to the fabric. One of the key advantages of pigment prints is that they do not need a final wash, cutting down significantly on their use of water. However, the fabric can lose its drape, while its particular feel – often called its hand or handle – can be altered because the pigment sits on top of the fabric.

In addition, the colour fastness and washability of pigments is not as good as that of dyes. Therefore pigments are most often used in small areas rather than all over, generally in products for fashion as opposed to interiors. Pigments would be less appropriate for flowing or semi-translucent fabrics as they would affect the flow and transparent qualities. However, the use of pigment prints on sheer window voiles is not uncommon; the design creates an interplay between translucent and opaque.

Pigments use fewer harmful ingredients today than they did 10 years ago, when chemicals such as PVC-based plastisol, kerosene, solvents and emulsions were used, and there has been a shift to water-based pigments. Other types of chemical pigment have been developed that react to a dyed ground to create contrasting colour effects with a better hand, saving energy and reducing environmental impact.

This one-colour pigment print by Clarissa Hulse, called 'Vine', is hand-printed on 100 per cent silk organza, creating a contrast between the opaque quality of the pigment and the sheer fabric.

DYES

Dyes contain chemicals that penetrate the individual fibres of a fabric and become part of it, unlike pigments, which sit on the surface of the fabric. There are many different dye types – reactive, disperse, vat, acid and direct – and each one is formulated to work with a specific group of fibres in order to provide optimum colour intensity and reliability. Dyes are more complex to work with, partly because they require thorough sampling; but the colour intensity and permanence is better than those of pigments, and the drape and hand of the fabric are unaffected. Therefore dyes are more likely to be used for full-coverage prints and for products where drape and hand are significant, particularly in the better or high-end levels of the market.

Table: A guide to checking which dye type is used on which fabric base and the fixing required.

TYPE	FABRIC	FIXING
Acid dye	Silk, wool, nylon	Steam
Direct dye	Cotton, silk, wool, linen	Steam
Disperse dye	Polyester, nylon, acetate	Steam
Reactive dye	Cotton, silk, wool, rayon, lyocell	Steam
Vat dyes	Cellulose fabrics	Steam
Pigments	All	Bake

Different fabrics require different types of dyeing; the same dyes used to dye a whole length of fabric, as seen here, can also be used for printing in a thicker viscosity.

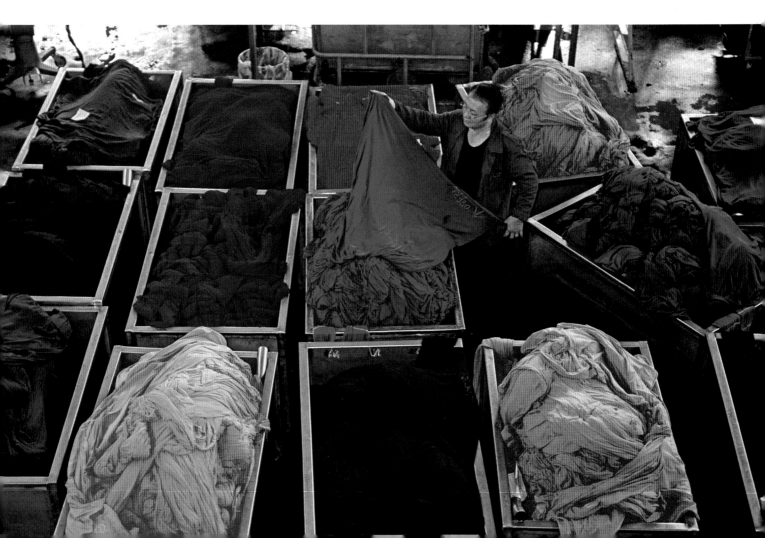

ACID DYES

Acid dyes are most commonly used on wool and silk but are also often used on nylon. These dyes can produce a good range of bright colours and can be used for dyeing, hand-painting or printing onto fabric. They are not particularly colourfast, especially when washed.

DIRECT DYES

Direct dyes are most commonly used on cellulose fibres and are called 'direct' because they can colour fabric without any form of pre-treatment. They are commonly used to dye fabric and can be 'discharged' and therefore used as a base colour. They are not often used for printing because they have poor light and wash fastness.

DISPERSE DYES

This dye type was developed in response to the growth of synthetic fabrics in the early twentieth century and can colour most synthetic fibres. They are the only dyes suitable for colouring acetate fibres and most polyester fibres, which must be dyed at high temperatures under pressure.

REACTIVE DYES

Reactive dyes are a popular colouration method with a market share of around a third. Developed in the 1950s, they offer a broad colour palette with bright tones and have excellent fastness on a range of fabric and fibre types. These synthetic dyes are used at room temperature and bond chemically to the fibre molecules, requiring the use of less water in the fixation process than many other dyes.

There are some environmental concerns in relation to reactive dyes' use of urea to support fixing during the steaming process. However, other chemicals are now available to replace at least some of it.

VAT DYES

Vat dyes are insoluble in water and require an expensive and complex process, but are often still used by high-end interior fabric companies and for the military, mainly because of their superior fastness to light and washing. They account for a small percentage of the dye market, however. Vat dyes were previously sourced from natural products, such as indigo, but are now mainly synthetic, and are best applied to cotton, linen and rayon.

PRINTING METHODS

There are three main methods used for the commercial production of printed textiles: rotary, digital and transfer printing. Each method has its own set of costs, advantages and drawbacks, and the design and function of your fabric will determine which print process to use. For example, the best print option for a swimwear collection made from high-performance synthetics such as polyester and polybutylene would be transfer printing. This is because transfer printing offers the high colour intensity that is a requirement of swimwear, while the disperse dyes used are highly colourfast to sunlight, chlorine and seawater, with minimal fading when they are printed on artificial fibres. On the other hand, a dense or heavy-pile fabric intended for high-market-level interior upholstery would achieve best results via screen printing to ensure even coverage.

Screen printing is often preferred for high-market-level fabrics for interiors, as in Dodie Sorrell's 'Wave and Spot' pattern, here printed on linen and also produced as wallpaper.

ROTARY PRINTING

Flat-screen printing developed as a production method in the early twentieth century as a process to print the emerging new art silk fabrics (rayon). The method was also being used by couture houses to print on silk and wool. These fashion fabrics required shorter runs than was economical for roller printing and a faster turnaround than could be managed by block printing.

By the mid-twentieth century it was possible to use a fully automatic flatbed machine, which moved the fabric one repeat at a time. This process is still used today, but has largely been superseded by rotary screen printing, which accounts for the largest proportion of global textile print production. The cost of rotary printing varies depending upon where the mill is located, the fabric base, the number of colours and any further supplementary finishing processes required.

Rotary screen printing factories are able to print up to 120 metres (131 yards) of fabric a minute. While the printing machines are very fast, the lead time needed to ready a print for production can be eight to twelve weeks. This is because pre-production processes include colour separations, repeat management, engraving the screens, colour matching and printing a strike-off (sample) for customer approval before proceeding to full production.

Rotary screens arrive flat-packed and are heat-treated to create their cylindrical form. To engrave the screen the most common method now used is laser engraving (the term 'engraving' is an overhang from when metal plates were engraved). This method uses digital information that has been developed in specialist software for each colour separation to 'engrave' each screen required to print the design. This method is fastest and most economical, allowing for fine detail.

An alternative method of engraving screens involves coating the screen with a light-sensitive emulsion. When this is ready it is placed on a rotatable copying machine and the full-size colour separation is placed on top of the screen. The exposure unit is turned on to set the time for exposure and to rotate the screen. The screen is then inspected for faults, which can be dealt with by painting directly onto the screen if necessary.

While the initial set-up is admittedly cost- and time-intensive, once completed it takes at most two days to print 10,000 metres (10,936 yards) of fabric. Although large orders of fabric can be printed quickly using this method, the increasing trend for short runs of less than 1,000 metres (1,094 yards) has meant that the advantages of this method are not fully realized for today's fast fashions and designs with their short lifespans. This is because the cost of making each screen (one for each colour) is significant, so the longer the print run, the more the cost reduces. The advantages of rotary screen printing include the ability to print more complex processes, such as discharge, resist, devoré, flock, relief techniques, metallics and pearlescent pigments.

With the increased demand for shorter runs, flatbed screen printing remains a significant manufacturing process because it offers a more economical and flexible approach. However, both rotary and flatbed screen printing have environmental ramifications. Screen printing requires resources including emulsions and coatings for the engraving of the screens as well as water for washing them, and produces a good deal of wasted printing ink.

Digital processes have been developed to reduce the cost and time involved in the sampling stage, and CAD systems can be calibrated so that the digital printers can offer an accurate sample of the eventual screen-printed production run. This helps to reduce the decision-making timeline before mass production using rotary or flatbed screen printing. Today's fabric printing companies may use some or all of these methods to manage expense, speed, volume and special requirements for their customers' print runs.

Textile production of a six-colour print on a rotary screen printer, which can print up to 120 metres (131 yards) of fabric a minute.

CASE STUDY
STANDFAST & BARRACKS

Standfast & Barracks is a fabric printing company producing fabrics for interiors and fashion, primarily on cotton and linen, using pigment and reactive and vat dyes for printing, as well as speciality effects such as foils and devoré. The print factory houses rotary screen and flatbed printing as well as digital printing, dyeing and finishing. The factory purchases raw, untreated fabrics (known as greige fabrics) from around the world and then processes them ready for print, producing approximately 80,000 metres (87,489 yards) of printed or dyed fabric a week.

Standfast & Barracks employs approximately 200 people, with around 20 people in the design studio. The studio designers not only create original designs to be sold to clients, but will also initiate designs from briefs or adapt and develop designs from a previously purchased design or archive piece. The design studio also supports brands and retailers in considering the most appropriate print processes, fabrics and dyes for their projects, as well as overseeing the interpretation of colour separations and screen engraving. The designers work with both traditional and digital processes, although all screen separations are completed by hand and then sent for digital engraving.

Once it has been approved, a new design is separated into the number of colours/screens required to print the fabric, and alternative colourways are created. Samples are then digitally printed onto fabric using textile-specific software that closely recreates the look of the screen print through the digital printing method. This provides the customer with an accurate impression of what the print will look like when printed by traditional methods in bulk production. When the colours are approved the design is sent to the factory where the colour technicians use a spectrophotometer (a tool that accurately measures light and thus also colour) to capture the colour data required for formulating the dye, which is then mixed in the colour kitchen ready for production printing.

At the same time, the design itself is laser-engraved onto rotary screens or transferred onto flatbed screens, and a sample run is then screen printed for the customer to approve before moving to production.

Once the fabric is printed, an enormous 'flash ager' develops the vat dyes and steams, washes and dries the fabric within five minutes. This enables Standfast & Barracks to check the colours and screens very quickly.

When the production is complete, finishes such as chintz or dirt repellents can be added before the fabric is pressed and put on a roll, ready to be checked by quality control.

Above top: The design studio at Standfast & Barracks, where two designers work on digital colour separations of designs. Note the magnification of the images on-screen to ensure that there are no stray pixels in the image.

Above centre: The colour studio: daylight bulbs are used to ensure consistent lighting conditions.

Above: Colour-matched samples waiting to be checked and/or sent for customer approval.

In general, the first production run is around 600 metres (656 yards). In the case of fabrics for interiors, this yardage is used to create fabric books that are sent to stockists for consumers to browse. Retailers and brands may initially request a run of 500 metres (547 yards) for each colourway and then begin to order more of the best-selling colourways at regular intervals. Standfast & Barracks stores the rotary screens until customers no longer wish to keep them, but this does mean that some remain in stock for at least 20 years.

With four rotary printing machines, two flatbed machines and four digital printers, the Standfast & Barracks factory covers a vast site. This scale of production is an indicator of the sheer volume of investment in materials, energy, knowledge and labour involved in the production of printed fabric.

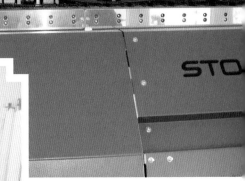

Above top: Digital printing is increasingly used for production printing as well as for sampling.

Above: This digital printer uses eight colours to give a full colour spectrum.

Left: Dyes are stored in the colour kitchen, where the recipes for colour mixing are managed by computer.

Above left: The 'colour kitchen' computer at Standfast & Barracks controls the distribution of the dyes into the dye vat, where the dye is mixed automatically to a good consistency. It is then tested for colour accuracy before being used in production.

Above right: The rotary screen printer can print up to 20 different colours, each requiring a separate screen.

Left: A two-colour print requires the use of two screens to print the pattern. The fabric is moving underneath as the screens rotate.

Right: Because flat screens are wider than rotary screens, the flatbed printing machine, which can print up to 21 colours, takes up more space.

Below left: As it moves along the conveyer, this 15-colour print is having the third colour printed.

Below right: Further up the same print table, the print is near completion as the 14th colour is printed.

INSLEY AND NASH

Fledgling textile manufacturers Insley and Nash describe themselves as a bespoke screen-printing company, and operate quite differently to a large producer such as Standfast & Barracks. Their business model is to offer a service that enables individuals or small companies to test their ideas in the marketplace or to produce short runs of printed textiles, using a range of print processes and more affordable set-up costs. Clients include designers, celebrities, and theatre and interior designers.

When launching their business, Insley and Nash recognized that there are still many print effects and finishes that cannot be achieved directly through digital printing – the most commonly used method for printing a short run of textiles. Their intention is to offer a new kind of print studio that is flexible and accessible, where they will work with clients on research and development to push processes forward, including post-production speciality effects on digitally printed fabrics. The main bulk of the company's work has used foils, matt foils, fluorescents and devoré – essentially the kind of processes that cannot be produced by digital printing – using acid, disperse, reactives and illuminants.

Right: The drying cabinet is a tent in which they place fan heaters for a short time to dry screens.

Bottom: A selection of the dyes and pigments used by Insley and Nash.

DIGITAL PRINTING

Digital printing has many advantages over screen-printing methods because of its speed, efficiency and lower costs for smaller manufacturing runs. Digital printing does not require colour separations or the engraving of multiple screens, so costs per metre, in theory at least, are the same whether you need to print 5 or 500 metres (5½ or 547 yards). At present, however, it cannot compete on costs at large volumes. Currently the fastest industrial-scale inkjet printers are capable of printing around 20 metres (22 yards) a minute, compared with a rotary screen printer that may process some 120 metres (131 yards) a minute.

Pre-production lead time for digital printing can be as little as two to four weeks as the only pre-production processes are colour matching and the printing of a sample for customer approval. The costs of dyes and inks, however, can be significantly higher than those of traditional printing methods. With ongoing research in this area, pigments have only recently been developed for inkjet printers, and this is likely to have a big impact on the future growth of digital printing. Inkjet pigments can also use an ultraviolet curing technology, which results in the ink drying almost instantly.

There are several digital printers that are capable of short runs of 50 metres (55 yards) and can typically print between 20 and 150 linear metres (22 and 164 yards) per hour at around 360 to 720 dpi. The best-known manufacturers are Dupont (Artistry) Reggiani (DReAM), Robustelli (Mona-Lisa) and Mimaki (TX2). There are now full production machines with 'roll to roll' production available to print between 360 square metres (394 square yards) per hour that are currently being released to the industry. While this still does not compete with rotary speeds of up to 1,000 square metres (1,094 square yards) per hour, the speed of printing is being advanced continually, and new inkjet printers running at 300 linear metres (328 yards) or 600 square metres (656 square yards) per hour at 1056 x 600 dpi and using water-based inks have recently been previewed by Durst Phototechnik AG.

Digital printing also expands the creative possibilities of design with its ability to print detailed patterns using any scale or repeat, as well as non-repeating or engineered designs, with no limitation on the number of colours used. This printing method will, in time, become the preferred print process for bulk production as well as for small runs.

Digital printing uses inkjets to propel dye or pigment onto fabric and has less environmental impact because there is less print paste residue, which in turn reduces the amount of water and energy used. Also, in theory, you can print only the areas required for use in the product and, therefore, reduce the ink coverage and thus the quantity of ink used.

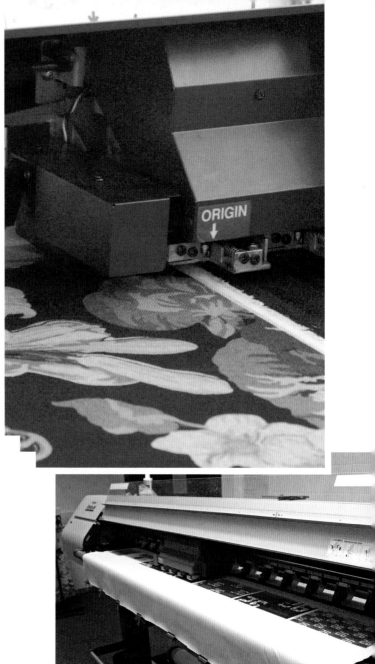

Controlled by a computer program, the printhead of an inkjet printer propels the dye or pigment onto the fabric.

FIRST2PRINT

Launched in 2001, first2print is a large-format digital print company located in New York and Los Angeles and is partnered with Design Works International, a design service bureau. The staff of 23 are experienced and knowledgeable about design, colour and printing, enabling them to support product development as well as the delivery of digitally printed fabric. The company's clients come to it for strike-offs and short production runs as well as for traditional or digital design services, special projects or design sourcing.

The company saw the need for US designers to turn around printed fabric samples quickly for prototypes, which would allow retail buyers to make quicker decisions regarding off-shore manufacturing commitments. With turnaround time for new ranges in-store decreasing to between two to six weeks, the pressure to produce printed fabrics more quickly has become an important driver. first2print has also become increasingly involved with supplying printed fabrics for short production runs for fashion, bespoke interiors and retail outlets, as well as for showroom and marketing samples, one-of-a-kind products and costumes. The company can produce a 23-metre (25-yard) run in seven to twelve days.

first2print uses a variety of digital printers, including Mimaki, Mutoh, Dupont and Encad. This range of machines offers the company flexibility across the 70 different types of fabrics and three dye types (reactives, acids and disperse) that it uses. The firm is happy to work on special projects that push the technology and may lead to a commercial advantage for both itself and the client.

first2print recognizes that there is some harmful chemical waste in all digital printing as it is 'printing on demand'; however, because the data for the specific garment is input into the computer, the amount of ink used is minimized as it does not need to cover the entire width of fabric. Its digitally printed photographic images of New York for the swimwear company Graffinis are an excellent example of the use of the technology to reduce waste, as the images are engineered directly into the cut of the suit, thus eliminating the printing of waste fabric. The reactive and acid dyes used by first2print meet Oeko-Tex® certification, an international accreditation system that limits the use of harmful chemicals.

Above right: first2print's web page shows the variety of textile printing and product application with which it is involved.

Right: This swimsuit for Graffinis was digitally printed by first2print; printing directly on the garment eliminates the wasteful printing of unused fabric.

TRANSFER PRINTING

Transfer printing maintains a market share of less than 10 per cent, despite a significant investment in this print process in recent years. The design is first printed onto paper with disperse dyes, either digitally or using rotary photogravure screens, and a full range of colours and tones can be achieved with these methods. Through the application of heat and pressure, the design is transferred directly onto the fabric in a process called sublimation, in which the solid ink on the paper is converted to a gas and then back to a solid again when it meets the fabric. A broad range of image types and qualities is possible, including digital and photographic imagery.

When printed on polyester or other synthetic fabrics, the disperse dyes used in transfer printing are extremely colourfast, making this process ideal for sports- and swimwear. The main restriction to this process being used more widely is that it is difficult to reproduce prints with enough colour saturation on natural fabrics.

Transfer printing is a reasonably economic printing process and can be considered less harmful to the environment than many other processes because there is less waste and minimal use of water. There are also no excess dyes nor any need for the application of steam or water to fix the fabric or to wash the screens. The main waste product is the paper that is used in transfer printing, which will often be recycled as paper bags or florists' paper.

This photographic-quality print by Paul Smith was produced by transfer printing on to synthetic fabric to be used for jackets and jacket linings.

SUSTAINABILITY AND DESIGN RESPONSIBILITY

In the fashion and textile industry there are many complex and varied issues that relate to sustainability and environmental concerns, and printed textiles are a particularly resource-hungry product. The production of fibres and fabrics consumes natural resources as well as using water and energy, while the use of dyes, colourants and finishes creates effluents that pollute the water supply. In addition, as a global endeavour the production cycle from fibre to fabric to finished product leaves an enormous carbon footprint. It is important that the next generation of printed textile designers is aware of these issues in order to ask questions and make design choices that will lead the industry towards more sustainable products and processes.

While making design choices regarding pattern, colours, fabrics, dyestuffs and manufacturing processes in the development of printed textiles, the designer is not only led by the design brief and cost factors, but by the need to accommodate the increasing demands for sustainability coming from the client or employer, which are ultimately driven by the consumer. These choices can result in a series of compromises that you might have to make in the design process. An understanding of the environmental pros and cons of various fabrics, dyestuffs and printing processes will guide you as you make these decisions.

You might find it is helpful to address these issues through the concept of 'design responsibility', where you as a designer consider how to prioritize and tackle some of the issues that are raised. Often, there are no easy answers or solutions to be found. However, beyond your choice of processes and raw materials there some additional areas that you could consider in order to contribute towards a more environmentally friendly industry: the reduction of waste and polluting substances; reducing the use of water and energy; and issues of ethical responsibility and slow vs. fast fashion.

Above right: Rachel Bending of Australian label Bird has tackled sustainability at all levels of the fashion and textile business: harvesting roof water and using a threefold system to flush waste water before it reaches the sewers; using water-based and azo-free dyes; and recycling fabric for a range of products, from fashion accessories to small-scale button covers.

Right: Small companies such as I Dress Myself produce limited-edition T-shirt prints with an ethical and environmentally friendly approach to print production.

THE REDUCTION OF WASTE

Printed textiles consume resources throughout their life cycle. The amount of waste produced throughout the cycle can be reduced through energy-efficiency schemes, particularly in the manufacture, travel and laundering of the textiles: reducing the amount of raw materials wasted, including dyes and other contaminants; reducing fabric waste through garment design; and discouraging the production and purchase of cheap garments that use up vast quantities of natural resources in their manufacture.

In addition, there is the question of the carbon footprint made by products travelling from one area of the world to another throughout all stages of manufacture and in relation to the supply chain. Many companies are finding economic as well as environmental benefits in sourcing closer to home, or locating the bulk of their supply chain in one region.

WATER

Another area in which there are moves to reduce waste is levels of water consumption throughout the processing of textiles. This begins with the high demand for water to irrigate crops, particularly cotton, and then follows throughout the production process in which steam and various methods of washing are used to fix and remove any excess chemicals from the fabric.

The need to reduce the use of water in the textile dyeing process is leading to new developments by chemical companies, including dyestuffs that can be fixed at lower temperatures, which can result in the consumption of as much as 50 per cent less water and energy. A completely waterless dye process that makes use of carbon dioxide (which can be recycled) is another recent development.

Holly McQuillan is a designer who has used the concept of zero waste to develop innovative fashion collections that do not waste any fabric..

CONTAMINATION

Of particular concern is the use of dangerous dyes and chemicals or their untreated effluents, which can contaminate the environment, especially the water system, and harm textile workers – these have been a significant issue for the textile printing industry for a long time. Legislation in many countries, particularly in the EU, now requires that companies reduce emissions, pre-treat effluents and dispose of colourants safely. However, in many parts of the world where labour is less expensive and manufacturing is less regulated, sustainable practices are strictly voluntary. Textile designers and retailers can choose to work with printers that adhere to good environmental practices.

A group of global fashion retailers and sportswear brands have joined forces with a goal of achieving zero discharge of hazardous chemicals in their supply chain by 2020. The 'roadmap' that they have identified will look at the chemicals used in the process, the needs of the product itself and the by-products of the process, such as the waste-water or sludge, in an effort to change the chemicals and processes used at every stage of the supply chain on a global scale.

ETHICAL RESPONSIBILITY

Issues of concern around ethical manufacture relate to the age, pay and conditions under which textile workers are employed. There are many organizations that work on a global basis to put pressure on both manufacturers and retailers to demand that their employees are not children and that their terms and conditions of work offer them a living wage, reasonable working hours and choices about whether they do overtime – similar to the working conditions that may be expected in a Western context.

Fashion designer Ada Zanditon aims to create innovative cutting-edge fashion that explores both organic and natural fabrics. She is committed to reducing and exploring novel 'energy-conscious solutions' in the development of her collections. Concerned with the provenance of the fabrics that she uses, she only sources from ethical manufacturers and ensures that she builds long-term relationships with them so that she can assured of their commitment to responsible production.

Ada is committed to minimizing waste reduction of cloth, recycling as much as possible. Within her design studio she attempts to make a difference in relation to energy consumption; cleaning materials and office stationary are also a focus, so that the ethos of responsibility carries throughout the business.

The number of businesses that take this approach is growing. However, because not all businesses take such positive steps towards more responsible practice, organizations such as Fashioning an Ethical Industry, Ethical Fashion Forum and Educators for Socially Responsible Apparel Businesses all exist to create awareness and encourage all fashion and textile businesses to consider how they could make more responsible decisions about their product development.

Left: A printed garment from Ada Zanditon's 'Poseisus' collection, which is made from organic fabric and designed to reduce waste.

Above: Ethical Fashion Forum aims to promote approaches to design, sourcing and manufacture of clothing which maximize benefits to people and communities while minimizing impact on the environment. It liaises with other worldwide organizations in the support of this aim.

SLOW FASHION

There are also ethical considerations around the lifespan of a product, such as how to maximize its wearable life or to ensure that its disposal is dealt with responsibly. While there is currently a strong ethos in fashion for throwaway and fast fashion, there are many designers who are attempting to challenge this by taking a different approach to the concept of 'fashion' and developing products their customers will choose to purchase and use for a longer time. Part of this approach is to celebrate craft, making and skills, and combine these with digital and other new technologies to make products that connect with people in a meaningful way. 'Upcycling', the use of discarded or leftover textile materials in the development of something new and beautiful, is also on the rise.

While slow fashion and upcycled products can be more costly, their intrinsic value will encourage consumers to enjoy them for a long time to come, and perhaps discourage the manufacture of cheap, throwaway products.

Tamasyn Gambell produces a range of textile products that are hand-screen-printed, using water-based dyes on luxurious fabrics. Tamasyn also produces a collection of upcycled scarves with materials sourced from a textile recycling plant.

DESIGN RESPONSIBILITY

The issues that are raised here offer an overview of sustainability and design responsibility within the textile industry. It is important to recognize and think about these issues in order to determine your responses, both as a designer and as a consumer. As a designer you need to establish which of these are most important to the client or employer, or to you personally, keeping them in focus as you make your design choices and deciding at which points you feel able to compromise.

The main decisions that you will make in relation to manufacturing a textile design concern fabric, printing process and dye type. Issues of sustainability might lead you to choose a fabric for which the manufacturer can demonstrate a transparent supply chain, document the impact of the production of the cloth on the environment and assure that it is manufactured in an ethically responsible factory. In choosing a dyestuff and printing process you may decide to establish which would cause the least environmental damage. The compromises you might have to make, however, could revolve around the cost and aesthetic of the fabric you choose, or the suitability of a dyestuff to a particular manufacturing process.

As this chapter has demonstrated, when it comes to the manufacturing of a textile design there are many decisions to be made that will affect the interpretation of your design onto cloth. Your relationship with the textile manufacturing process will depend upon which type of design role you move into, but understanding the complexity of your design's journey from when it leaves your hands to the moment the final product is realized will help you make a number of decisions. It is also important that you understand the process as a whole so that you can recognize that the fabric, dyestuff and printing method each have an impact on how the design is experienced by the consumer. Sustainability issues will present significant design challenges for the next generation of designers.

All designers develop their own working methods, which may determine the context in which they choose to design. The next chapter looks at a selection of designers and their individual approaches to designing and addressing the many choices to be made in developing their printed textile collections, including the various employment opportunities within the industry.

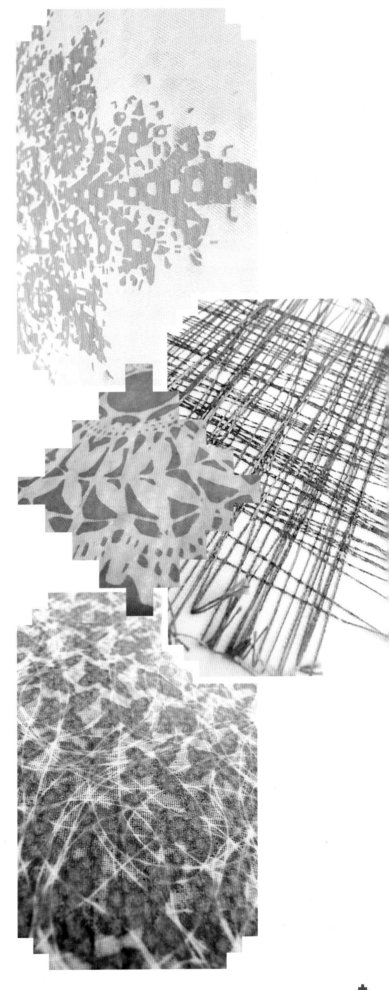

Kate Goldsworthy's project has involved new tools and finishing techniques to design recyclable, aesthetic 'surfaces' within the context of a 'closed cycle polyester economy'. The materials used are 100 per cent recycled polyester and the finished works are fully recyclable with the ECO CIRCLE® system, a patented system for breaking down used polyester products that can then be re-polymerized into virgin-quality materials.

5
DESIGN IN PRACTICE

INTRODUCTION

Becoming a designer of printed textiles requires focus and determination; it is a competitive field. How you choose to practise printed textiles will affect your level of interaction with decision-making processes and your influence on the final outcome. That is why it is important that when you are studying textiles you try out different ways of working so that you can establish what is the best choice for you.

The definition of the printed textile designer's role will be set by a particular company's approach, and its level of flexibility will depend on the company's size, vision and role in the supply chain. In general terms, the larger the company, the less opportunity you have to engage with all of the decisions involved in getting a product to market. A larger company will tend to have a larger market share, which is likely to mean that they will have tried-and-tested routes to product, whereas a smaller company may be more likely to innovate and take risks.

You may decide, of course, that you wish to be in control of all of these parameters and make your own decisions on the critical path from idea to product. If so, working within a company might not be appropriate for you, and you may find it more rewarding to set up your own business. Textile designers working in industry tend to be anonymous; the company name or designer that they work for is usually the one that is acknowledged and promoted and, in a fashion context, is the identifiable 'star'.

Your aspirations might also stretch to developing a business venture to design and manufacture textiles under your own label, or becoming a designer–maker working on your own handmade products. Many designers design their own print collections and integrate print into their products in innovative ways. Celia Birtwell, for example, worked in the 1960s with fashion designer Ossie Clark and has recently produced new collections for Topshop as well as under her own name for interiors. Designers such as Angie Lewin and the late Lucienne Day have captured the interest of the public with the vintage appeal of their interior fabrics.

Previous spread: Vallila Interior is known for dramatic statement prints. In this design by Tanja Orsjoki for the 'French Visits' collection, large-scale photographic imagery and bold block colour focus attention on specific areas of the design.

This page: Sian Zeng's innovative interactive wallpapers enable the user to alter the story by adding speech bubbles or new characters from a selection of magnetic elements.

Another possibility is that you may be drawn to textile art applications or to work in community or gallery contexts. The skills and knowledge that you develop in the process of your design training may also mean that you can apply them in a range of creative industries: fashion forecasting, working as a colourist, buying, merchandising, fabric sourcing, print production, retail management or teaching.

The following range of examples and case studies will enable you to see how some designers have made choices in their practice. This will offer you a view of various employment and self-employment opportunities, and some of the day-to-day business aspects typical of these different paths.

Above top: Celia Birtwell came to prominence in the 1960s through her collaborations with fashion designer Ossie Clark; she continues to design for fashion and interiors, as well as accessories. This collection, called 'Mystic Daisy', is for interior fabrics and comes in several different colourways.

Above: The work of St Jude's – a company initiated by Angie Lewin – has sparked an approach to textiles that is less trend-focused while also ensuring that the designer is acknowledged in the process.

Right: Lucienne Day produced inventive designs, many of which have become design classics. In the 1950s she led a new approach to printed textile design, moving away from the essentially floral-driven textiles of the time.

FREELANCE DESIGNERS

Many textile designers are freelance or self-employed, creating collections to be sold at trade fairs or directly to clients. Some represent themselves, building up lists of clients for whom they work regularly. They will often forge strong relationships with specific manufacturers and retailers, and may sometimes be involved with development of designs for manufacture. Others work for a design studio or agency that promotes the work of several designers. In this case, once the design is sold the designer is no longer involved, and spotting a design on a passer-by may provide the first glimpse of the finished product.

It is possible for freelancer designers to work with an agent, who takes on the role of liaising with industry, selling, managing financial negotiations and dealing with copyright issues. Designers in turn will regularly send work to the agent to promote on their behalf. Working freelance often requires you to spend a lot of time working in isolation – as a lot of designers who do this work from home they have to be well motivated and focused.

Freelance designer Davinder Madaher produces interior textile designs for a range of retailers as well as printed textile designs for fashion.

CASE STUDY
LINDA THACKER

With a degree in surface pattern design, Linda Thacker has worked both as a freelance designer and a design manager for a wallpaper company. As a design manager she became involved in technical developments for substrates and finishes within the company's research and development department. This role allowed her to develop new methods and approaches to developing products.

However, Linda found that in her role as manager she missed the more hands-on design work, and moved to another wallpaper design company for whom she now works on a freelance basis. As a freelance designer her involvement is varied and may include styling a whole collection, designing a new collection or adding to an established one, or overseeing the manufacturing process.

Linda's skills and knowledge lie in an understanding of the market for high-end fabrics and wallpapers and an expert knowledge of their manufacture, while also having an ornate, detailed handwriting. She now works, from her home-based studio, directly with manufacturers and brands to develop collections for GP & J Baker, Zoffany, Sanderson and Harlequin.

Recently, Linda developed a collection of strié wallpaper with Zoffany – a luxury interior design brand. The process for creating the strié involved the removal of colour from a surface with the use of a brush, leaving a soft and subtle striped effect. Zoffany wanted to produce a collection of wallpapers using this effect to work alongside its new paint collection.

For this collection, Linda was given a set of Zoffany paint colour chips with which she began to create mock-ups of colour combinations showing how she could work the colours together, developing a range of colour combinations with a traditional feel, as well as creating additional options for a younger palette. Two of the more contemporary colourways were influenced by fashion collections, one from an Alexander McQueen purple-and-gold colour palette and another from a Chanel advert using matt and gloss black.

Feedback from the company was that the combinations were working well; it then decided to develop the wallpaper collection further using an image from its archives. The stripes were proofed with initial prints that were checked for print and colour quality, and then developed further and the individual colourways selected.

Above top: Linda Thacker works in her home-based design studio for a variety of manufacturers and brands.

Right: The wallpaper at the bottom, 'Eugenie', was designed by Linda for Zoffany using a strié effect, creating a subtle striped background with a damask print on top. Above are two colourways – black and grape – of 'Malmaison', which uses palettes inspired by fashion-design advertising. Both designs are from Zoffany's 'Strie Damask' wallpaper collection.

Linda's working methods have changed over the years. She started initially with visual research from which she developed the design ideas, leading her to think about layout, repeat and the final design. With experience she is now able to think in a slightly different way: she completes her visual research, photography and drawing and then, using her own photographs, objects, archive material or books, she is able to develop images with a sense of the style and effects that she is trying to achieve, beginning to work and think about layout, organization and structure far more quickly.

Linda uses both tracing paper and CAD to work on design elements during this process. She works mainly with linear qualities so that she can focus on organization of the imagery and the relationship between positive and negative space. Linda also develops what she refers to as a 'technique sample', for which she takes a section of the design and works with the details of the image, textures, surface qualities, colours, shades and tones; this is then sent to the screen engravers as reference.

Essentially Linda does not produce designs in a traditional manner; she produces a layout and a detailed visual example of the imagery, relying on the separation artists who work in the manufacturing studio to put this together and separate the colours in preparation for manufacturing. This is essentially a 'shorthand' method of working between design and manufacturing and comes only when there is a trusting relationship between the company and the designer.

Above top and above centre: Linda uses a range of resources to inspire her design process, including design magazines and a library of information from previous projects. Design development for her 'Hummingbird' artwork is included here.

Above: This 'technique sample' is an example of the work Linda produces and submits to her clients, along with the full repeat layout of the design, which is usually on tracing paper.

CASE STUDY
ANA SANTONJA

Ana Santonja has her own studio in Barcelona called Demandingmass, in which a small group of designers collaborate across a range of markets, professions and contexts to ensure stimulating careers. Ana produces textile designs, has a digital printing bureau and teaches textile design, as well as producing an annual pattern design publication. This type of mixed economy is common with textile designers – it offers security of earnings as income is made from several sources and the variety of projects offers a range of stimuli. Ana exhibits at events such as Heimtextil and Indigo, but she also engages directly with clients, who will often give her a brief to work from.

Ana describes the skills required to be a successful textile designer as creativity, courage and determination, combined with luck. While Ana's business requires lots of energy to keep so many diverse areas working effectively, she says that she loves the creativity and freedom that this diversity allows her.

Above: Ana designs everything in repeat – generally at 64 x 64cm (25 x 25in) – and never uses more than eight colours in her designs. She follows these guidelines unless she is commissioned specifically to work to a different specification.

Left: Ana's designs can begin in various ways – she often draws with traditional media but usually designs everything digitally. She always has an end product in mind when designing, although customers often use her designs for other purposes.

Below: Ana exhibits regularly at international trade fairs, where samples of her work on the walls and tables invite clients to sit and look through the collection with her.

DESIGN STUDIOS

Design studios offer original and innovative design concepts that manufacturers and retailers can purchase and will then use in order to build their own design collections. You may work in a studio where you are producing designs for a particular brand as well as designing and producing products as a supplier for other retail brands. In both of these cases it is likely that you will spend the majority of your time developing your own original design ideas rather than developing and altering those that have been sent to you by clients.

The studio is likely to provide resources such as a library of books and magazines, print and dye facilities and sewing machines. A studio manager may allocate specific projects to particular designers, or greater freedom may be given to individuals to respond to trends.

Taylor McArdle is a fashion-led design studio, working almost exclusively on fabric. It has facilities for printing and dyeing textiles as well as for computer-aided design.

CASE STUDY
COLORFIELD DESIGN STUDIO

Colorfield Design Studio is based in London and New York, with the design activity in London and the New York office focused mainly on selling. The art director is based in the London office and works closely with a design manager who oversees the design studio, which is staffed by nine full-time designers complemented by two freelancers.

Colorfield sells an approach and attitude to design that its customers respond to. The company sees itself as a fashion-forward design studio, with clients as diverse as Kenzo and K-Mart. It focuses on fashion, though it has sold designs to interiors companies, and develops two main collections a year – spring/summer and autumn/winter. Important selling events are trade fairs such as Indigo, which is held twice a year in September and February at Première Vision in Paris, where the company expects to have at least 400 designs in its collection.

The sales team has developed a core customer base; they see around six customers a day and generally see each of their customers on a monthly basis. The communication between the design group and the sales office is important and they are in daily email contact; the design team receives specific information about what is selling well, and the designers are given comments on their work, which helps them focus on the next group of designs.

The design work begins by analyzing the catwalk shows and developing mood boards for shape and colour, in December for spring/summer and May for autumn/winter. The designers participate in a weekly design studio meeting, when everyone brings in magazine tear sheets, photos and books to share. All of the designs are created as flat, two-dimensional garment shapes developed with a range of digital and hand processes. Each designer designs two-dimensional shapes and photographs them before they are sent to the USA. In the studio on a Friday afternoon before the designs are sent to New York, a lot of furious stitching and photography takes place.

Above top: At Colorfield Design Studio, designers and the sales team are in close communication regarding designs that are selling well; here a designer is working on a collection of florals.

Above: Pre-mixed dyes are set out in the Colorfield studio so that the designers can keep the colours consistent across a collection while it is in progress.

 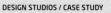

The studio focuses on four main groups of designs at a time, each of which has around ten individual designs in it. Each designer is expected to produce around ten designs a week, so on average the London office sends around a 100 designs a week to the USA. They also send photos to New York on a daily basis so that everyone is aware of how the collections are developing. The US office sends back daily reports of sales, in particular the 'hot cakes' that are proving most popular, so that they can build on that success. The company also produces a text-based summary for each season, which is given to its regular customers.

Colorfield's designers are on a basic salary plus commission on a sliding scale, depending on how many of one's designs are sold. They have opportunities to travel abroad and to go to selling fairs or on sales trips, as well as occasional trips to galleries and exhibitions thought to have an impact on design trends. The designers generally enjoy the fast pace and structure that the studio offers. The staff is well established, with the majority being employed for over five years, though they have recently appointed three new graduates. The company also offers internships of two to three weeks, which usually involve supporting the designers, assisting by preparing and completing tasks, or putting together swatch books or mood boards.

Above top: Colorfield presents all of its designs on two-dimensional fabric samples that are shaped to suggest a garment; these are sent to the sales office in the USA at the end of each week.

Above: Using a CAD program, a designer in the Colorfield studio develops a collection of geometrics.

CASE STUDY
ANNA NELSON

Anna Nelson is a designer in a small company that sells designs in the UK and internationally to independent retailers, high-street chains and catalogue and Internet retailers. She works in a team with four other designers and three merchandisers/buyers; the designers oversee technical production within the whole team, and the managing director oversees activities and assigns design briefs. Anna's position requires her to spend 50 per cent of her time on design, 30 per cent handling production issues and 20 per cent dealing with administration or attending meetings and getting feedback from the sales team.

Beyond the design qualities of having a good sense of colour, imagination and visual awareness, Anna also employs good drawing skills, a commercial awareness, computer skills, a good understanding of repeat and technical knowledge of how her designs will be printed.

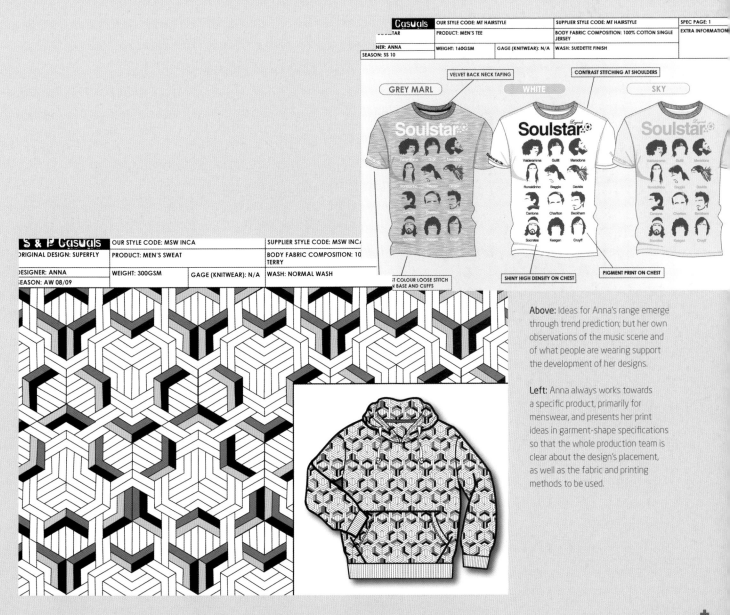

Above: Ideas for Anna's range emerge through trend prediction; but her own observations of the music scene and of what people are wearing support the development of her designs.

Left: Anna always works towards a specific product, primarily for menswear, and presents her print ideas in garment-shape specifications so that the whole production team is clear about the design's placement, as well as the fabric and printing methods to be used.

DESIGNER-MAKERS

A designer–maker is likely to have more control over manufacturing the fabric and may also oversee production for a company. These responsibilities offer a wider opportunity to influence the end product right through from initiating the design work and organizing the manufacture of the textile or product to the maintenance of the product's quality and selling it directly or through retail outlets and online sales in order to develop the brand.

Emma Moloney is a printmaker who produces a range of different products including wallpaper and wall-hangings. As a designer–maker, she is involved in the whole process of designing, producing and marketing her work.

CASE STUDY
TIMOROUS BEASTIES

Timorous Beasties is an internationally renowned design duo that creates challenging and dynamic conversational designs and is a leader in the high-end wallpaper and interior fabric markets. When designer Paul Simmons graduated with his MA in 1990, he was frustrated by the potential jobs available in the interior textiles market. With his partner Alistair McAuley he established Timorous Beasties as a non-traditional design company with the freedom to produce its own fabric, wallpapers and interior design products.

As a small start-up they could not afford the large production runs that established manufacturers would offer, and decided to create their own studio. While working to establish their brand, they found that persuading retailers to stock their unique work was difficult, and eventually they launched their own shops.

Setting up their own studio and selling through their own retail shops have allowed Timorous Beasties to become more experimental in its design techniques. The company's designs have moved from naturalistic impressions of insect and plant motifs to a modern, slightly subversive interpretation of historic French toiles, and the duo continue to stretch their design skills by combining hand printing with new technology.

As a product- and process-driven designer, Paul believes that it is part of his role to work with compromises; he finds it more interesting to work within restrictions, such as using one screen and one colour, which challenge his design skills and push him to produce something different.

Paul is interested in history and collects all sorts of things: ceramics, silhouette portraits, prints, books, woodblocks and books on natural history. These serve as a library for his ideas. Paul does look at what other designers are producing, although he tends to focus on furniture and products rather than textiles; he also tends to look at concept-led designers such as Matthew Hilton or Droog.

Paul had the idea for his well-known subversive toiles in his head for some years before he felt it was the right time to begin to develop it. That collection brought together all sorts of things that interest him – drawing, traditional print elements and history. The toiles attracted a lot of press coverage, which increased sales and also led to Timorous Beasties' nomination for designer of the year in 2005, organized by the Design Museum in London.

Paul works on computer in the design development stages but feels that it is important to maintain control over the process. He feels it is lazy to resolve a drawing or painting merely by mirroring. His working process involves drawing (often with pen and inks), scanning, printing, reworking and scanning again.

For Paul, drawing is an extraordinarily important process and he feels strongly that to be a good print designer you need to

Above top: Timorous Beasties is interested in playing with concepts and appropriating them within a different context. In 'Grand Blotch Damask', a motif reminiscent of a Rorshach ink blot is controlled and developed into a damask-style design.

Above: The simply drawn image of a moth is repeated and used to create a structured design of circles and floral shapes.

Left: Printed here on a 3-m (118-in) panel of wool voile, this design has also been produced as wallpaper and as lace.

put in the time to draw. He draws to capture the qualities he wishes to explore, while considering the requirements of the screen or digital process and keeping in mind the limitations of colour or scale.

While he is not trend-driven, Paul does think looking at colour trends is helpful in light of the company's retail sales. He recognizes that interior products can be expensive and, therefore, people will be living with them for some time. Paul believes that his customers tend to buy products that relate to their own personal references and what they know, and therefore colours for new products need to work with those already in the home.

The range of product types that Timorous Beasties now produces requires him to consider how an idea is going to work on fabric for upholstery, walls, ceramics and cushions. All of these products require a different response and consideration of form.

The workflow of the company's year demands quite a structured approach as it tends to launch its new collections at key annual events: Milan Design Week in April, New York's International Contemporary Furniture Fair in May and the London Design Festival in September. The entire process, including design, sampling, final designs, product applications, photography, writing promotional information and uploading to the Internet, takes the best part of a year. In the summer months the duo focuses on producing products to sell in its shops in the lead-up to Christmas.

With success has come expansion: current demand for Timorous Beasties' products requires it to run the print studio in two shifts and to outsource some production; and there are plans to add an e-commerce facility to its website. It also works on commissions throughout the year and is currently working on a design for a whisky bottle, a limited-edition cushion for a large retailer and a New York toile design.

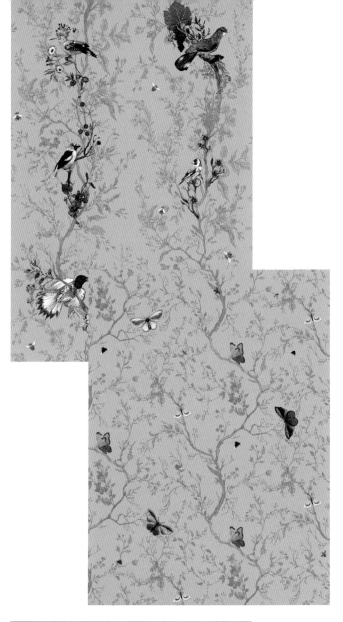

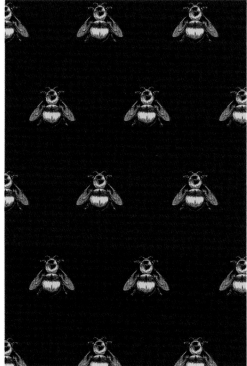

Above top and above: Seemingly drawn from natural history archives, the collection, including 'Birds and Bees' and 'Butterflies' shown here, creates drama with the appearance of full-colour motifs against tonally camouflaged branches in the background.

Right: This simple one-colour drawing of a bee is printed at larger-than-actual scale, disconcerting the viewer. The drawing and detail are characteristic of Timorous Beasties' style.

CASE STUDY
SIDE FIVE

Side Five, a three-person design studio in Madrid, produces and distributes its own fashion and home collections, as well as stationery and wallpaper, has a catalogue of exclusive prints that is constantly evolving and develops designs and illustrations for its clients. Designers Gredilla Lucia, Elisabeth Aranda and Patricia Fernandez met while studying for an MA in Pattern Design and Surface Applications, with previous studies in fine art, fashion and architecture. They believe this combination of backgrounds gives their company a fresh quality as they have different and complementary ways of looking at concepts.

While they naturally focus on their customers, visiting clients and creating new opportunities for business, they also recognize the importance of communicating and developing strong relationships with their suppliers while continuing to consider more competitive opportunities. The designers also devote time to research, ensuring that they follow specialized press and keep up-to-date with developments in the area of printed textiles in terms of manufacture, design, fabrics, colours, etc.

Their research also includes meeting with colleagues in the arts and cultural arenas to promote the exchange of ideas, as well as looking for inspiration in terms of cultural travel and keeping alert to new trends and the contemporary zeitgeist. Much of their travel time is also spent in visiting trade fairs to sell their designs and meet new clients.

The group believes that the combination of being able to draw and a strong sense of colour is vital to good design. They also recognize, however, that understanding scale and proportion and considering texture in your design and its application onto fabric are equally important. Technical skills are also vital, especially being in control of digital tools rather than being overly seduced by what they can do.

The group's ideas come from travel, museums, magazines, books, trends and trade fairs; or sometimes they are commissioned to produce designs based on a particular concept. Side Five's collections build from an intial inspiration, from which its members develop a concept, and then a colour palette, before beginning the design process. They try to find particular details and information to differentiate their work and make a collection unique, always working with the final outcome in mind to ensure that they come up with an appropriate result.

In particular, Side Five relies on the individual tactile qualities of fabric, and the impact of these qualities on the design's interpretation. The studio feels that its engagement with the relationship between the design, the fabric and the final outcome is a vital component of its success.

Side Five produces a range of designs that are varied in style and effects, including simple 'tossed' motifs or highly structured geometrics or florals. The designs are intended for a range of different markets and end uses.

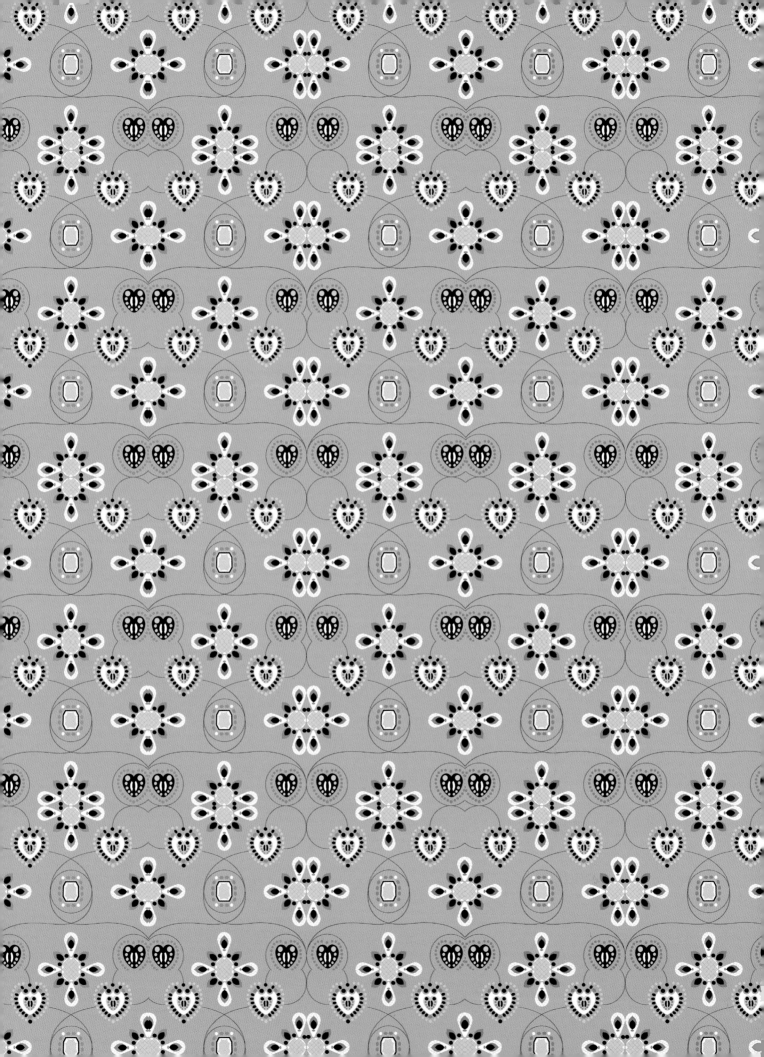

TEXTILE MANUFACTURERS

Textile manufacturing companies usually employ designers within a design studio environment, initiating new design ideas or developing collections that may be pitched to clients. In-house designers may also develop ideas that have been passed on to the manufacturer by retailers or brands, who may have purchased artwork from a freelance designer or studio. Separation artists or employees with more technical expertise may also work there, developing their clients' design ideas into the colour separations, developing colourways and even sampling the print, working with the client until the print goes into production.

Left: The members of Side Five met while studying for their masters degrees. Because they all have different backgrounds, including fine art, architecture and fashion, they all bring a different set of skills to the Madrid studio.

Above and right: Textile manufacturers that develop their own collections, such as Prestigious Textiles, will often consider the entire range of fabrics for interiors, as here for the 'Art & Soul' collection, spending time styling these interiors for the benefit of retailers and consumers.

CASE STUDY
LUCY WILHELM

Lucy Wilhelm, an Austrian designer who studied printed textiles at university, was offered an opportunity to work for the Italian textile manufacturer Friulprint as the result of winning the International Talent Support competition in Trieste early in her career. Established 30 years ago, Friulprint was one of the first companies in Italy to specialize in digital print, and produces for high-end and luxury designer labels as well as for international high-street labels.

Lucy worked on two successful collections for Friulprint spanning the spring/summer and autumn/winter seasons. She was able to develop her own brief and to oversee the entire project from initial concept and colour specification to the creation of final designs and repeats. She also attended Première Vision with Friulprint, which gave her the opportunity to speak to clients and respond to customer demands.

Working in a design studio situated within a busy textile manufacturer enabled Lucy to develop a broader knowledge and understanding of the print process and to consider how to use this experience to further enhance her design skills. Working in an Italian company selling to global brands also helped her to understand how to develop a broad collection that has international interest. She now works for a leading global brand based in Germany, working on print collections for menswear and womenswear, and enjoys the process of designing for a brand with an established identity.

Lucy considers that the key qualities for establishing a career as a designer are passion and stamina. Understanding colour, shape, fabrics, repeat and how to use CAD programs are the critical skills needed. She also believes it is necessary to learn how to behave professionally, as people can be very direct in their comments about your work, and you must respond to criticism in a positive and constructive manner.

Lucy feels that it is essential to have a clear idea of the ultimate application of the design – whether it is a T-shirt or a duvet cover – as that will affect the selection of colour, shape, size and materials. While she has a strong handwriting and design style, she understands that it may not always be suitable for the client and so works to ensure that her style does not overpower the collection. She strives to be objective about her work, believing that one's favourite colours, subject matter or layout are not necessarily going to fit with every trend.

Lucy's working methods often come from her gut instincts, developing her own perspective on the trends she sees around her. She researches social and political trends, the worlds of film and music and reads a lot. After sketching out her ideas she begins to gather visual information and colour options, as well as looking at what other designers are doing and working out their sources of inspiration. She can spend up to three weeks doing both primary and secondary research – drawing, taking photographs and trying out new techniques by hand and on the computer.

From this research, Lucy develops a mood board to inspire her while developing her collection. She works primarily through digital methods, scanning in her drawings and photographs, layering and building compositions and images that work together. She considers scale and proportion as well as the colour palette that she defined at the outset.

Lucy talks about applying critical judgement – the process of understanding what is working and what is not – as being an evolving journey, where the views of others are crucial to supporting your analysis of the quality of your designs.

These designs by Lucy Wilhelm are from three different collections developed independently to be sold as fashion prints at events such as Indigo at Première Vision. Without an actual product or market level in mind, Lucy focused on responding to market trends in terms of colour, imagery and scale to ensure that the collections were saleable. The designs at the top and centre right reflect an interplay between drawn and photographic imagery with their use of florals and natural imagery. Those at the centre left and below show an abstract exploration of scale and motif with a less natural use of colour, along with an interest in the exploration of cell-like structures.

TEXTILE CONVERTERS

Textile converters purchase or create designs for conversion into apparel or interior fabrics – developing ranges and presenting them to manufacturers or retailers, and then organizing their production. While converters do not own manufacturing facilities, they purchase greige fabric and arrange to have the fabric printed, finished and delivered to their customers. Converters often use print facilities all around the world and have built relationships with them; their choice of print manufacturer depends on the print process and the costs associated with it. Designers working for converters may often be involved in sales; they may also oversee production.

Angel Textiles is a New York fabric supplier offering the services of its creative design studio as well as two fabric and print lines ('Angel' and 'Plum') and an extensive vintage archive. The fabrics are woven in Asian mills and printed in Korea. The Plum line, shown here, is young and modern in attitude, offering playful prints and a range of unusual fabrics.

CASE STUDY
MOLLY FRESHWATER

Molly Freshwater set up Freshwater Textiles in 2007 as a design and sourcing company for mid- to upper-end high-street retailers that require the involvement of a designer to support the conversion from design to final product, ensuring that the aesthetic of the collection is maintained.

Molly works across several different brands, primarily on bedding and 'top of bed' products. In many cases she works on a design-only basis, while for some brands she also offers a sourcing service. Her relationship with clients may extend into brand analysis, reporting on trends and areas on which to focus their brands. She also takes some collections through to promotion, packaging and photography.

When creating a collection for a customer, Molly produces a mood board and works on design ideas either by hand or digitally. These design ideas are then shown to the company and, on approval, are made up into concept samples. When the concepts are approved, Molly writes a design specification outlining the colours, fabric and materials to be used in manufacture. Samples are then produced and final decisions are made; a purchase order is then placed and sent to the factory. Delivery dates are established and production samples are exchanged for approval. Packaging is also commissioned at this stage and ideas are developed for styling and graphics.

As a converter, Molly does not own any printing or manufacturing equipment. She is responsible for purchasing the greige fabric and overseeing the production of the finished fabric with manufacturers which may be in other parts of the world. The flexibility of her business allows her to offer her clients a choice of services, from original design and development through to production.

Molly has established good relationships with two factories – one in India and one in Portugal. In India the textiles are hand screen printed with a wide range of print processes; the company also offers hand finishing including embellishment and embroidery. Molly uses the factory in India for smaller production runs. For her bulk production she uses a rotary screen printer in Portugal that can manufacture runs of 5,000 metres (5,468 yards) plus. It can print up to 16 colours, although Molly does not generally produce designs with more than four or five. Here she works mainly in pigment, printing on cotton fabrics. When making decisions about fabric, process and dye type, she is influenced by the need to deliver the product for sale within a specific price band.

Currently Molly is a sole trader, though there are occasions when she employs two freelance designers. Her role, therefore, includes attracting business, marketing and sales, designing, administration, production management, testing and packaging.

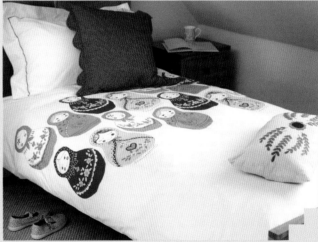

These two bedding ranges were designed and manufactured by Freshwater Textiles for Feather and Black, which retails both bed linen and bedroom furniture. The designs demonstrate an interest in contemporary takes on tradition for adult bedding and in nostalgic imagery in fresh colours for children.

GARMENT SUPPLIERS AND RETAILERS

Garment suppliers act very much like textile converters but instead of producing only fabric they will also oversee the manufacturing of the end product, often in their own production facilities, including delivery to their client's warehouse or direct to store. Most department stores and high-street brands also develop many of their own products, and will employ printed textile designers as part of their creative teams. While these jobs can be very corporate in nature, they offer an opportunity to influence products that will arrive on the retail floor, and to connect with the consumer in a meaningful way. Each brand or store will have a different approach and signature style, which the printed textile designer must be able to understand and translate successfully through the design process.

S&P Casuals is an international business with offices in the UK, US, Germany and China. As a successful import/export and wholesale business it has in-house design teams and garment manufacturing. This enables the company to supply its menswear and boyswear products to a wide range of international retailers.

CASE STUDY
ANNA PROCTOR

Veteran print designer Anna Proctor's first position was working with a company that essentially sold fabric on from textile printing mills, mainly in Turkey, to UK-based retailers. Anna was the first designer that the company employed and her role was to liaise between the mill and the retailers to help shape the fabric designs that were being produced into something that would sell in the UK. The mill had large markets in Russia, Germany and other regions and produced a varied portfolio of fabrics. In this role Anna did not initiate designs, but bought designs from freelancers and then reworked and re-coloured them to suit the customers before sending them to the mill. The role included a lot of administration, meeting with retail buyers and travelling to the mills in Turkey.

Eventually Anna joined a garment manufacturer that supplied a number of major retailers. Anna was the only print designer in the company and liaised closely with the fashion designers to develop appropriate print ideas, as well as meeting with the buyers to learn about their objectives. As in her previous role, she bought designs from freelancers and studios and re-worked them. In addition, she oversaw the engraving of screens and the actual print production. She built up a strong relationship with one of the retailers, creating a successful collaboration in which she was involved with most of the print designs for one of their collections for two years.

After a stint as a freelance designer, Anna joined a major retailer as its design manager. This middle-market, large company has several labels under one umbrella company name. She described this as a very corporate environment where there were 30 fashion designers and five print designers, as well as a colour specialist who worked on all aspects of colour, responding to trends and developing palettes, as well as managing the standardization of colour across a range of fabrics and products. They all worked closely together and met on at least a weekly basis to ensure that the building and completion of design collections was developing in unison.

The print team was responsible for responding to the company buyers' requests along with initiating and developing its own design stories. Each quarter, both the fashion and print design teams for each label were required to present their ideas to the other designers and buyers, as well as to the leadership team. Working a year in advance, this would include trend overviews, key themes and mood boards, colour palettes, fabric samples and print concepts. While the outcome of these meetings was a consensus about the new collection, it was expected that changes would occur as the catwalk shows and other events influenced the season's direction.

The design team in this context was a creative one, and in a large company like this the manufacturing aspects of print production were handed over to dedicated staff. Anna's experience and ability to talk about the production process and ensure that the designs were appropriate for production led to smooth relationships between suppliers and the manufacturing team, with less 'snagging' in the process.

Above top: Anna Proctor's experience and design flexibility are evident in these two designs from her freelance collection. A freelance textile designer, particularly one working in fashion, must be able to adapt to any new trend that emerges.

Above: This collection of visual images combines a range of similar trend ideas with some of Anna's own doodles, functioning as a mood board and demonstrating Anna's thinking process while she develops a collection based upon the trend.

CONTRACT FURNISHINGS

Clients for contract furnishings are often architects or interior designers developing a collection for a business such as a cruise ship, a hotel, hospitals or a chain of restaurants. The design brief for these projects may specify a wider and more technical set of criteria beyond colour range and design style. An office environment, for example, might require particularly hard-wearing fabrics with specific performance requirements for laundering, sanitation, noise reduction, temperature control and flammability. A textile designer for contract furnishings will need to design with specific criteria in mind, and may need a more technical knowledge base.

Contract furnishing companies such as Skopos need to ensure that they produce designs that have both a contemporary feel and aesthetic longevity, as their designs will be in place for a longer period than might be expected of a domestic interior.

CASE STUDY
STEPHANIE JEBBITT

Stephanie Jebbitt is a designer who has worked in a variety of design studios and is now self-employed, producing design solutions for both home and contract environments. One project, described here, required her to design a textile suitable for the interior of a new specialist hospital for children. The brief outlined a design that would create calm, harmonious surroundings, linking the outside rural setting to the interior of the hospital, and that could be adapted to suit both psychiatric and medical units.

To meet the technical performance standards required in such a setting, a polyester fabric was specified that could be laundered to medical standards, was treated with an antimicrobial finish, draped well and had a natural appearance. The print process to be used was transfer printing.

Following the brief, Stephanie took her design inspiration from the rural landscape and made a series of studies of the countryside, concentrating on the colour and formation of landscape and on the horizon between the sky and land at different times of day. Stephanie created designs that were non-specific in motif, avoiding complicated images that might create the effect of busy, crowded areas when used as cubicle curtains or drapes at windows. She ensured that the design repeated across the width of the cloth, and used stripes as vertical effects so that making up and joining the widths would be practical and simple.

For her palette, Stephanie studied healing colour theory and created alternative combinations of colour suitable for surgical wards, burns units, maternity wards and mental health areas. For example, lavender is recognized as a calming, healing colour and, when combined with other soft tones, is suitable for use in maternity and post-surgical wards. Blue tones are cooling and are often used in burns units.

Stephanie's design process started with a series of landscapes painted in watercolour and in mixed-media collage and resist. She then engineered these images using different repeat methods to experiment with scale and balance. This process was carried out digitally using CAD, and alternative colourways were produced across the five designs that were selected for the collection.

During the development of the design, Stephanie met the architect to discuss the brief and the key objectives that were required to create the desired effect in her fabric. She took colour references from materials used in the interiors, including the flooring and walls, and studied the artist's impressions of the building to understand what the environment would look like. Lastly, she presented full-scale prints of the final textile designs in repeat, and produced samples of fabric for approval with complete independent certification, demonstrating that the fabric would perform to the critical standards of safety and performance required in a medical environment.

Above top: In answer to her brief, Stephanie Jebbitt produced photographs, watercolours and prints of rural landscapes as her visual research, developing their colours and marks to suggest representational effects using blue tones.

Above: As the collection developed it became more abstract, the colour fresh and calm, with soft effects in the mark-making. This suited the requirements of the brief to create a calm, harmonious environment.

DESIGNING FOR NICHE MARKETS

Besides designing prints for use in fashion and interior textiles, there can also be interesting opportunities in designing printed fabrics for what are often described as 'niche markets'. These niche markets tend to be within very specific areas of manufacture, such as sports or swimwear, lingerie, or even in the automotive industry.

Lily Rice graduated with a degree in performance sportswear. Her collection is built around the concept of stripping away excess to create innovative pieces that are informed by the structure of the athletic body. Lily has used print to echo the geometric shapes suggested by the forms themselves.

CASE STUDY
MARY CRISP

Mary Crisp trained as a textile designer in a variety of commercial settings, including interior collections, although she now specializes in designing car interiors (see page 115), working as a studio designer for global car manufacturers in their colour and trim departments.

Each project that comes in to these departments is given to a group that might include a textile designer, a graphic designer, a decoration parts designer and a project coordinator. The group receives a briefing from the marketing department to the exterior team, then on to the interior team and finally to their team.

The colour and trim department designs every colour, material and texture for every surface of the car, usually taking around two years to complete a project. There are specific moments in the development of the project when the team presents all the concepts to the board of directors for approval.

Mary's job requires that she is aware of global design issues – some of the biggest emerging markets are currently China and India. The team tailors the cars especially to these markets, including their exterior, interior and materials.

Mary's role is to support the existing demands for textile design but also to expand and develop new concepts; she has been developing original printed, embossed and embroidered concepts for some future car models.

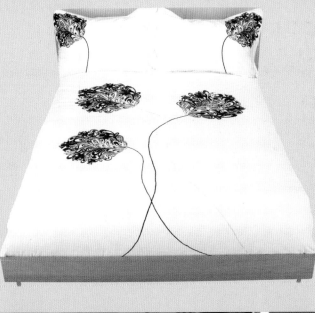

Above top: A peony motif, machine-embroidered on 100 per cent cotton, for a UK retailer.

Above: These heat-fused digital prints on vacuum-formed plastic lights formed part of Mary's masters degree course.

Left: As part of a corporate rebranding project with the Victoria & Albert Museum, London, Mary Crisp developed a collection of designs inspired by the museum's William Morris archive.

CRAFT PRODUCTION / TEXTILE ARTISTS

Many textile designers, particularly those who are interested in following their ideas through from initiation to the final product, become interested in self-employment in craft or as a textile artist. This way of working gives you control over all the production values and the design of your product range, as well as a direct relationship with your consumer, particularly if you are interested in selling your work directly through craft and design markets. Working for yourself is not an easy option and the set-up costs can be formidable – these will include paying for a studio, printing facilities and production. You may be able to find grants that are available from governmental arts associations or from charities; universities also often have incubation units to support initial set-up.

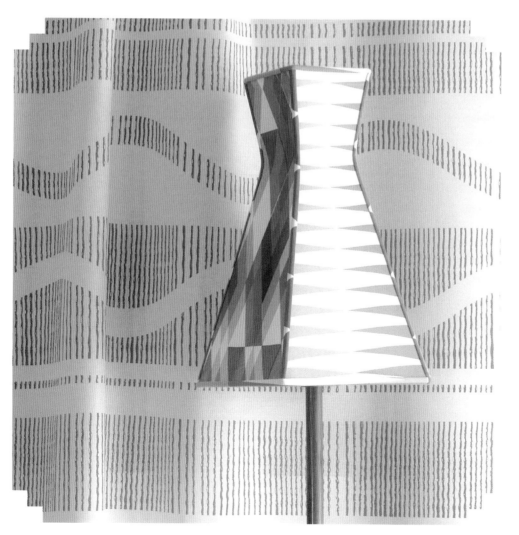

Screen-printed by hand by Marian Lynch of The Colourhouse, this design uses water-based pigment pastes on organic cotton sateen, applied to a metal frame and hand-stitched. This traditional soft-furnishing technique has been used here in a contemporary way.

CASE STUDY
TERESA COLE

Teresa Cole, who trades under the company name of Teresa Green, is an established designer–maker who both sells her range of products at craft and maker fairs around the UK and has established retail customers. Teresa has her own illustrative style of simple line drawings, which in general explore natural life and rural pursuits. Her product applications are related to home textiles, accessories and, more recently, children's fashion. Teresa set up the business with initial funding from the Arts Council and The Prince's Trust (a fund to support young businesses), and this enabled her to purchase a printing table, screen-wash facilities, screens and squeegees.

Teresa has always enjoyed producing linear drawings, using pen-and-ink and adding interest with variations of line quality and weight. She realized early on as a student that the way she enjoyed working was through exploring visual imagery with her own style, as opposed to being under pressure to churn out designs to fit trends or restyle existing ideas.

Teresa develops one main new collection a year, which she launches each autumn at the large design fairs held in London. Her work is sold throughout the UK, as well as in Europe, Japan, the USA and Australia. She prints all of her work herself, valuing the fact that each piece will be unique because it is handcrafted. She makes some of her own products but also sends some to UK companies to manufacture in order to support local industry.

Teresa appreciates her self-employed status, though she also does some teaching on degree courses as this gives her an opportunity to work with other people, enabling her to think about things in new ways. She enjoys the flexibility her situation offers, as well as the trade and craft fairs that contrast with the time she spends in the studio.

Above top: Teresa Cole's print workshop – she has a range of screens on hand for immediate use depending upon the scale of the product.

Above right: Teresa printing tea towels which, when finished, are dried on the washing line above her head. Using this method she can print small batches at a time.

Right: Teresa's signature style is illustrative, with naive, simple and fresh qualities. She develops her ideas in her sketchbook before considering how they might be applied to her growing range of products.

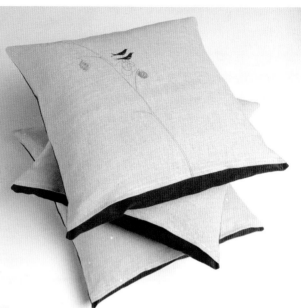

Examples from Teresa Cole's range, which embraces a wide spectrum of home and interior products, stationery and garments.

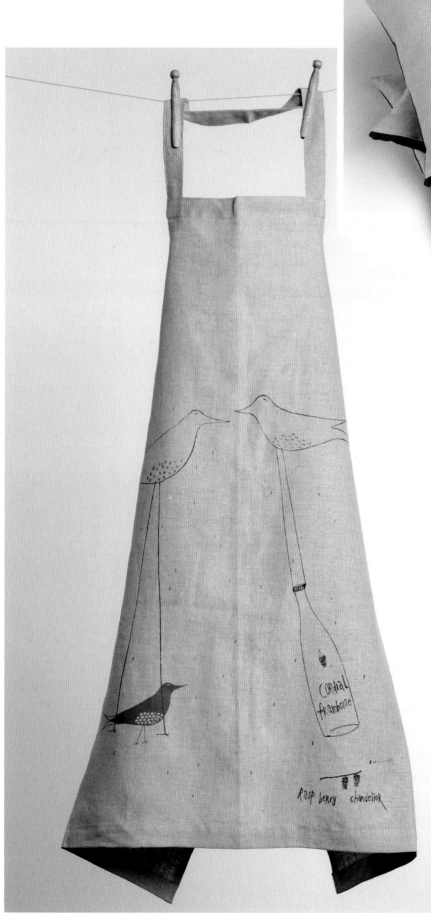

Cordial framboise

Rasp berry chandelier

CASE STUDY
DAWN DUPREE

Dawn Dupree studied Fine Art Textiles at Goldsmiths College, London, graduating in 1989. Dawn refers to herself as a textile artist, a title she acknowledges has some difficulties with definition. Within six months of graduating she applied for and was awarded a Crafts Council grant, which enabled her to find a studio and purchase items such as a print table and screens. The Crafts Council also offered support and direction, giving her an opportunity to receive feedback that was crucial to her success at this time, as her work was dynamic and exciting but often unresolved.

Dawn decided to establish herself by launching at a large event where she could get maximum publicity and feedback. She applied to the Chelsea Crafts Fair, which she saw as an investment in her business because it was a venue visited by buyers from galleries that might offer shows to her in the future. The process of getting ready for this event opened up a lot of questions for Dawn about scale, products and pricing. Dawn mainly produces wall hangings and panels; while she produces some interior products she does not get too close to being a designer–maker. The largest pieces that she has made were four-metre (14-foot) lengths for the British Embassy in Moscow; but she tends to work in one-metre square (four-foot square) dimensions, as this size lends itself to a more commercial application.

Dawn's work is not at all led by trend or design – she works mainly with concepts or through her own thought processes. For a long time her work considered the urban landscape and she took photographs of objects that she found in the streets, or of empty buildings and vacant lots, using the atmosphere they created as a 'stage set' around which to build a story. Currently she is working with eggs and nests, which relate to her personal experiences of family life now that one of her children has 'flown the nest'. A voyage to South Africa by sea reinforced the concept of empty or temporary dwellings. Working in this way, making connections between seemingly disparate events, inspires Dawn to create narratives that engage the viewer in her work.

Dawn feels that you have to be determined and flexible and that you need to have self-belief, as life as an artist can be insecure. She tries to show work nationally or internationally around three to four times a year and likes the feeling of the deadline as this gives a structure and focus to her work. As far as working practices are concerned, she stresses that it is important to be vigilant about other people copying your work. This has happened to her on a few occasions, but has always been rectified without the need for serious action.

Dawn Dupree's print studio, where she develops and produces all of her artwork.

She adds to her income, and breaks up what can sometimes be an isolated existence, by teaching textile printing in several institutions; she enjoys the diversity this gives to her working week. She also teaches her own short printing courses at various locations, sometimes linked to an exhibition where her work is on display. Dawn is presently re-evaluating her work and developing a new direction for her prints. She is keen to engage with more site-specific practice and work more collaboratively with artists from other disciplines.

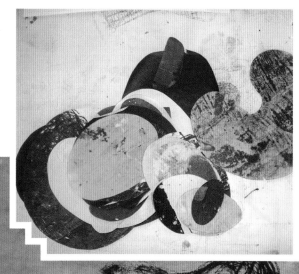

Dawn Dupree has her own working methods: she photographs, draws and develops her ideas to the point where she can begin to 'storyboard' them. Her designs are multilayered in terms of both image and print processes. She puts imagery photographically onto screen but also uses paper stencils for printing or to block areas out to protect them from printing. The print below, called 'Maternial', developed from ideas about her children having flown the nest.

USING YOUR OWN DESIGN APPROACH

The designers showcased in this chapter all have a particular relationship with textile manufacturing, either in terms of how their designs go on to be developed or through their own direct engagement with the printing of the textiles. Much of this depends on the area in which they choose to work, and the design approach that works best for them. For example, Linda Thacker uses her technical knowledge of printing processes for wallpaper and interiors, along with her unique handwriting, to develop her images with the style and effects she is trying to convey. For Paul Simmons, drawing is critical, while the print processes he references, such as the historical toiles, have significant impact on the aesthetic qualities of the design. For both of them, practice and experience have resulted in the ability to draw and develop imagery simultaneously.

The designers of Side Five look to the relationship between fabric and print to develop their concepts, while staying focused on fulfilling the design brief. Lucy Wilhelm takes plenty of time for visual research, using a mood board, and then works primarily through digital methods to develop her imagery.

Designers working in large design studios, such as Colorfield, may be disconnected from their eventual customers and end products, while those working for brands or retailers, such as Anna Proctor and Mary Crisp, are part of a large team dedicated to a specific product or customer base. A very personal approach and some eclectic influences characterize the work of independent craft designers and textile artists, who enjoy the hands-on experience of creating one-offs along with running a business.

A designer's approach to design and working methods is developed over time and is highly individual. While there is no right or wrong, you will find that your own approach may influence the type of print designer you become, and the role you choose to practise within the industry.

This design is from the 'Beautifully Brutal' collection by Lisa Anne Wilkinson, which uses hand-printed industrial rubber tassels. Her approach explores non-conventional materials, such as manipulated printed rubber, alongside fluid, hand-dyed and printed cloth.

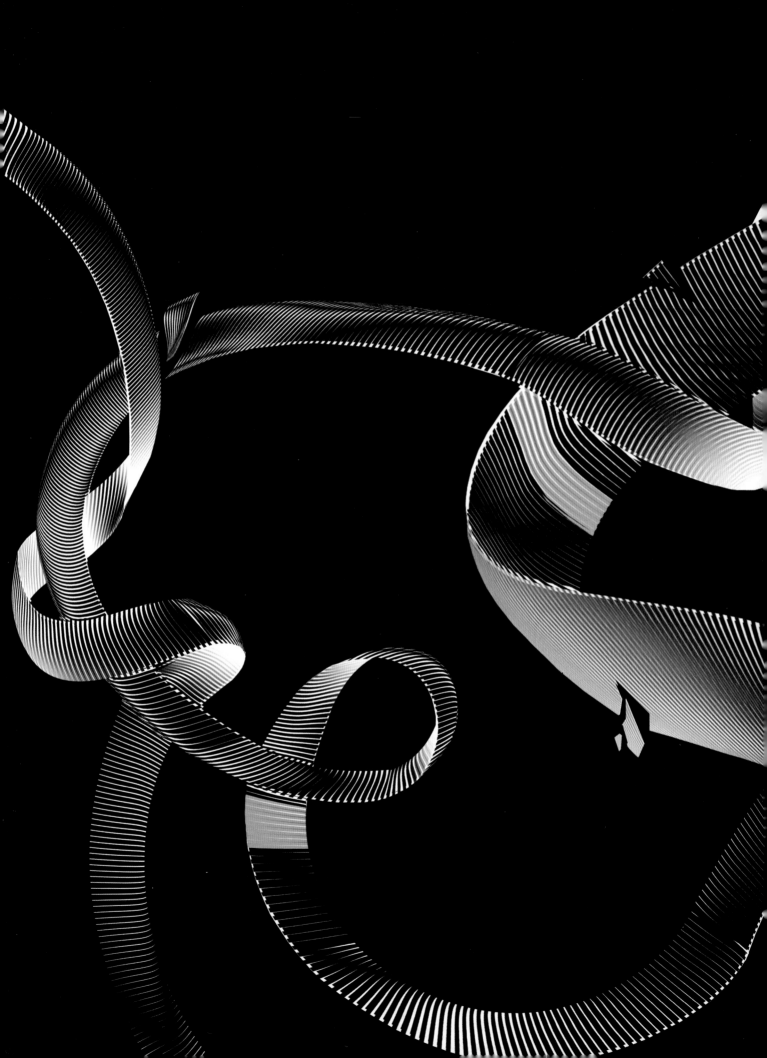

6
BECOMING A
PRINTED TEXTILE
DESIGNER

INTRODUCTION

The previous chapters have considered the full range of skills and knowledge that printed textile designers need in order to practise successfully. This includes an understanding of the context in which they work and the fundamental design skills that are required, as well as the techniques used to begin to develop those design skills in the print room or through digital methods, and the ramifications of the various options in raw materials and means of manufacturing. With time, a designer develops the confidence to make these choices and critically assess the results in terms of fulfilling a design brief and creating a design collection.

Sometimes the demands of time, new markets, product or style may take you in new directions and challenge your ability and skills, forcing you to ask new questions about how to approach your design brief. Ensuring that your approach has some flexibility and that you are not afraid to try something new is crucial to expanding your horizons and will lead to your becoming a good printed textile designer.

Previous spread: Kit Miles designs avant-garde prints for interiors that combine scale, colour and imagery with an architectural context.

This page: This fashion print by Sarah Patterson from her Folded Geometric Collection combines a variety of shapes in different sizes with a tonal, moody colour palette, which is freshened by the use of opaque pastels.

THE DESIGN PROCESS AND CRITICAL JUDGEMENT

Your design brief should outline the parameters of the project – the concept, the context, the product application, the colour palette, the market – and may also include information about how the design is to be manufactured, or the type of fabric. The visual and contextual research that you focus upon will, therefore, be based around these requirements.

The next stage in the process is to consider how you are going to produce your design collection. As you begin to develop experience, knowledge and understanding of the processes that you need to enable you to realize the design ideas to the required standard, it is likely that you will develop your ideas through a combination of photography, drawing, consideration of textures, digital work and exploration in the print room, along with market analysis, trend research and investigating a broader context of the subject.

At this point you must select, edit and refine your design ideas by making decisions about which elements are effective and require further exploration and which need to be dropped. This process relies on your development of critical judgement in order to ensure you meet the aims of the brief while producing something that is both aesthetically and technically resolved.

Developing critical judgement takes time, and you might find that talking through your design development work with other design-focused people is helpful. Taking time to offer feedback on other people's design work will also help you to develop critical judgement. By doing so, you will learn that anyone commenting from a constructive and objective viewpoint is able to assess strengths and weaknesses and, thus, when people comment from such a point of view on your work they may spot things that you yourself had not noticed. Practising these skills in college tutorials offers a structured environment for you to develop your confidence and your abilities in this area, and in turn enables you to make more effective decisions.

Visual research by Georgie Worker explores both painterly and linear media. Georgie has captured the fluidity of flowers as they begin to droop and age, and is also using colour to suggest the ageing process.

THE DESIGN COLLECTION

Your design collection is the result of your work and the fulfilment of your design brief; it may have been developed for a client, or for your own portfolio. A collection is a term used to describe a group of designs with unifying and cohesive characteristics, such as colour, style, use of fabric and print processes; but these designs should, in general, have different motifs and images. This is particularly pertinent if you want to sell each individual design from your portfolio. If designs appear too similar, or have repetitions within them, then those buying them may ask you to remove other similar designs from the portfolio. You can think about a design collection as being like a family – they have similar characteristics but none of them looks exactly the same.

Some designers or studios refer to a whole portfolio of designs produced for a season as their collection, but generally you may refer to a group of designs of around six to ten as a collection; you might have several groups of this size in your portfolio. Having enough visual research to use in a collection is vital, as you need to ensure that you have enough variation of imagery so that your collection does not become repetitive.

Finally, it is important to recognize that you need to translate your imagery from your drawings into designs and not merely apply those drawings to a textile. This translation procedure, trying out various approaches to print processes, scale and repeat, organization, individual motifs, compositions of different elements, texture and colour, will constantly challenge your skills and critical judgement, and is at the heart of your practice as a printed textile designer. All designers have a personal perspective and will develop their own working methods as they translate and progress through drawing, developing images, pattern, repeat, digital methods and print processes, creating a personal style or handwriting and making each collection of printed textile designs unique.

Katy Aston's graduate project shown opposite is an interesting example of the start-to-finish development of a collection with a very personal perspective.

Above: Jo Bedell's inventive approach to detailed representational drawing has a surreal quality. Exploring such angles at an early stage of your project will enable you to add an extra layer to your design collection.

Left: A more abstract quality has been sought by Louise Grant in this painterly floral.

Below: Jodie Harfield's drawings of nudes and flowers have led to a representational collection, which is further enhanced by some coordinating designs of simple geometrics.

CASE STUDY
KATY ASTON

Katy Aston is a graduate of printed textiles whose innovative and dramatic final collection of seating and cushion concepts was both process- and product-driven. Katy decided to focus on a conceptual project that would challenge the viewer through its use of image and surface qualities.

In this project Katy wished to construct her own imagery instead of embarking upon visual research through drawing. She was inspired by a process of conceptual thinking that emerged as she watched the major urban regeneration and redevelopment in her home city. She was fascinated by changes to the structure of the city each time she returned for a visit.

Katy also wanted to explore the transformation involved in moving from three dimensions into two; generally you would work in two dimensions and continue to translate your imagery through two dimensions. The objects that Katy wished to use – wooden blocks, dolly pegs, cocktail sticks, pencils – were easily recognizable but they also reflected, in an abstract context, the changing urban landscape that inspired her. The objects could be used in isolation or in groups to abstract them, allowing her to look at them in a variety of different ways.

Katy decided on the colour palette very early on in the project as she planned to paint her objects before photographing them. The colour palette of grey, black and brown, with a few brights and pastels, was inspired by the journey she took from the city to her home past the building works.

While wanting to inject some three-dimensional aspects into her designs, Katy's desire to innovate through her use of processes drove her project. She wanted to work with embossing, digital printing and hand painting, as well as the heat press, in order to create tactile imagery.

Her choice of fabric was important for the realization of these dimensional qualities in the surface, as well as for enabling her to explore post-digital printing methods: working into the print with water before it was steamed, as well as embossing the fabric by using a collograph printing press. She experimented with a range of fabrics and found that velvet was a good substrate to work with because it captured the colour well, absorbed water well enough to enable her to work on top of the print and also presented the embossed qualities at their most dramatic.

Katy Aston used recognizable objects as the starting point for her project. After establishing her colour palette, she painted the objects and photographed them in groups, creating patterns, shadows and structures for her to develop further.

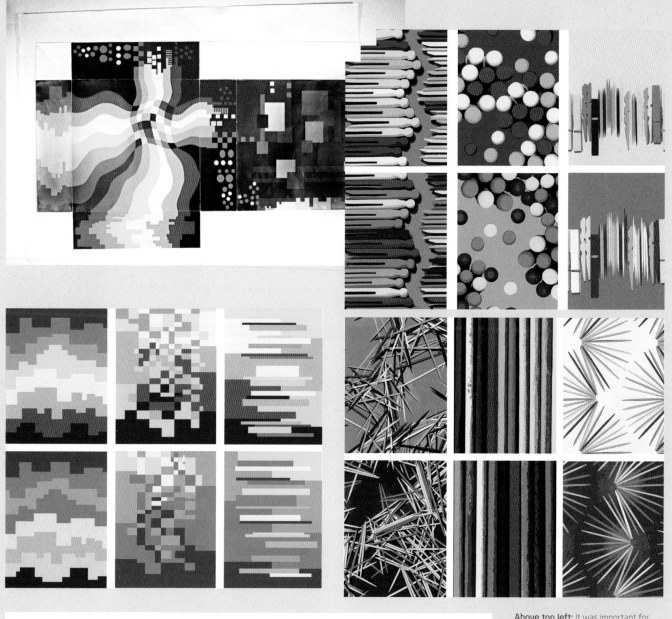

Above top left: It was important for Katy to consider how her designs would move around the square and rectangular modular seating ideas she developed. She printed out her designs on paper and turned them into cuboids to help her to understand the effect the form had on pattern, and to visualize how the two-dimensional designs could be developed into three-dimensional products.

Above: Katy developed several collections, one of which was representational of the objects, another involving repetition of pattern, and another that abstracted solid structures to explore scale and proportion.

Left: Some of the designs from Katy's collection as final products.

WORK EXPERIENCE

There are decisions that you are likely to make during your course or programme that will result in your focusing on a particular career path among a range of possible design applications, including apparel, accessories, soft furnishings, upholstery, wallpaper, illustration or surface pattern. One way of finding out where you might fit in is to undertake work experience or an internship during your course, which may continue afterwards. Work experience can be extremely beneficial as it gives you the opportunity to put into context the things that you have been learning, and to understand their relationship to the real business of printed textile design. Giving yourself a variety of experiences in a range of different studio environments is also useful to gauge best what suits your personality and approach, and can really boost your confidence and inspire you to succeed in your chosen career. Work experience can also give you concrete experience to put on your curriculum vitae (CV) and to talk about in an interview.

First, you need to consider the kind of company where you might like to gain work experience. You may find that your course has links to design-related businesses, or lists companies that you could approach. You could also find company names from trade-fair listings on websites, or use business listings in libraries or on the Internet. Start with retailers or brands that inspire you. Some may have websites that include information about applying for an internship, or you can ring the head office and ask. Take the time to find the name of the person you need to contact – it demonstrates initiative and enables you to make a personal link. You will probably need to write to several companies when trying to attain a placement. Try not to be deterred by a lack of response or a refusal; the key to a successful career in many areas is determination, and printed textile design is no exception.

Often placements are unpaid, but some will pay a contribution to your daily expenses or offer a flat rate for a week. There are also many design studio opportunities available internationally, and many students go to Italy, France, Denmark or Australia to work in studios and with manufacturers.

During your work experience, it is helpful to keep a diary and make note of all the activities that occur in the studio and in the daily life of a designer. Talk to the design team to find out more. For instance, how many designs do members produce in a week? What media do they use? Where do they get ideas? How do they use trends? You may also consider how the studio is organized. How and when do they sell and to whom? How do they put collections together? Do they have meetings to which all of the designers contribute? This sort of information will help you later when you have interviews by reminding you of the detail of the placement.

It is also important to impress the team you are working with, show initiative and, where appropriate, take on responsibilities. Building a good relationship with the company and thinking about what you achieved can help if, at a later date, you want to apply for a job there. If you make a good impression they might offer you a job when you graduate. If you are keen to develop your relationship with them further, then personally inviting them to your degree show or any other exhibitions that you are involved with is a good idea.

PROMOTING YOURSELF AS A TEXTILE DESIGNER

As a designer you need to promote yourself, and this can be achieved in a variety of ways. To begin you will need a portfolio, a CV and a covering letter. It is also helpful to have developed business cards, postcards, a digital portfolio or a website by the end of your design course.

PORTFOLIO

Your portfolio needs to demonstrate your skills and abilities as a designer by showing your best work in a professional and clear way. The size of your portfolio depends upon your work and you should choose this appropriately. Mounting work for a portfolio can be completed in a variety of ways, but here are a few golden rules and some useful guidelines.

◆ Your mounts should have equal borders to the left and right, while the bottom border should be deeper than the top one.

◆ Your design work or fabric must be cut with straight lines and perfect corners.

◆ Your portfolio must always be in a professional and clean condition.

◆ Ensure that the portfolio starts with an extremely strong piece of work.

◆ Use good-quality white cartridge paper (unless there is a good reason not to), as anything heavier will make your portfolio too heavy.

◆ You can protect your design work by using clear tape on the back and then placing double-sided sticking tape on top of the clear tape. This allows you to change your mount without damaging your design if it is on paper.

◆ Only attach your design at the top.

◆ Try and keep the flow and direction of the imagery the same, working in either landscape or portrait format (the latter is preferable).

◆ All paper designs should be presented in the manner illustrated here, while fabric swatches should be A3 or smaller.

TIP: A GENERAL RULE OF THUMB IS TO INCREASE THE SIZE OF THE MOUNT TO THE NEXT SIZE OF PAPER, FOR INSTANCE AN A2 MOUNT FOR AN A3 DESIGN.

◆ If your design is too big for your mount and your portfolio then you should consider folding it back on itself so that you don't see the back of the paper or fabric.

◆ There are other ways of mounting fabric samples. One method is to cut a line in the mount through which the fabric is pushed and then taped at the back. The other way is to use a light card 'header', which is folded to sandwich the fabric in-between.

◆ Don't hem fabric samples. Use an iron-on adhesive web, such as Bondaweb®, or sticky tape, such as Scotch® tape, on the back. Use a ruler to draw a straight line, and cut samples with sharp scissors; buy a pair of fabric scissors and keep them for this purpose only.

◆ In general you should avoid using plastic sleeves for textile portfolios because there are often tactile elements that those viewing the portfolio would like to be able to touch.

◆ You need to be selective about what you put in your portfolio; don't be tempted to include everything.

◆ Always organize and plan the order in which your work is going to be viewed.

◆ Ensure that you can talk about the work, but equally, be prepared for your portfolio to be considered without your commentary.

◆ Printed textile design work can be presented in a range of sizes. CAD work tends to be A4, A3 or A2, whereas hand-developed work can be 16, 32 or 64cm (6, 12½ or 25in) wide for textiles or 52cm (20½ in) wide for wallpaper designs. Mounting this work on the next-largest size of paper is the general rule. If you have a portfolio that is A1, however, do not have mounts smaller than A2.

◆ Your portfolio may include drawings, mood boards, design development and final designs. You can also include some evidence of CAD, repeat and visualizations of your designs in context. Early in your career, taking along a sketchbook is also a good idea.

DIGITAL PORTFOLIO

Increasingly, graduates are spending time developing digital portfolios of their work for distribution on CD. Each design will be labelled with the concept name of the particular project, and will include the same items as a physical portfolio: a mood board, drawings, colourways, design development, final designs, visualization, and so on. Below are some guidelines for the creation of digital portfolios.

◆ You can add text, keywords and any specific information about a project, such as market, trends, process and fabric types.

◆ Think very carefully about the organization of your presentation and the colours you use. Ensure that all the spellings and grammar are correct. You can also personalize your portfolio with labels that feature your designs and contact details, both on the CD and on its container.

◆ Since your digital portfolio is going to be viewed on screen only, you should ensure that the resolution of the images is at screen-viewing size – no less than 72 dpi.

◆ Try to ensure that you only send or give these CDs directly to people from established companies and don't leave them unattended at public events.

◆ If you intend to send your digital portfolio by email to a company to view, ensure that the file size is manageable and will not block their inbox.

Creating promotional CDs enables you to put together a visual journey of a project, enabling people to see your skills and thought processes as you develop it. It is important to ensure that this is presented professionally and says something about your aesthetic values and judgements.

WEBSITE

There are several websites, such as www.moonfruit.com and www.mrsite.com, that offer templates to enable you to develop your own web presence by outlining your portfolio, your career aspirations and contact details. While some are free, others charge a fee or require you to purchase a software package. There are also sites, such as www.artsthread.com, that allow graduates to upload a digital portfolio that may be viewed by a database of members from the industry looking to recruit new talent. If you choose this option, it is worth looking at several sites and comparing their various terms and conditions before committing yourself.

If you are interested in developing your own site, you can register a name (known as a domain) for the site (your own name, or your company name if you are going to have one). There are many sites available on the Internet that will research the availability of the name that you have chosen, and charge you to register and use this name on an annual basis. You also need to develop the kind of information or content that you wish your site to communicate to your audience. Websites tend to have 'pages' that each hold a collection of information, which can include items in the following list.

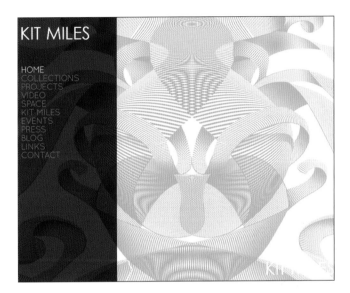

◆ **Home** – Your opening page, which needs to be visually interesting. It needs to make clear what you do. Are you trying to promote yourself for employment, promote a service or sell products?

◆ **About** – This is where you give an overview of who you are, your design approach, your aspirations, what you do and what you hope to do.

◆ **Portfolio** – This is where you can show design work, drawings, inspiration, mood boards and so on (see page 194). You should include whatever you think is relevant and interesting to your audience, making sure your message and objectives are clear. Your work should be small-scale and at low resolution so that people are unable to download it and use it directly.

◆ **News** – This can include regular updates on where your work has been seen, any press that you may have received and also any successes that you have had.

◆ **Blog** – You can keep a blog where you can give your followers updates about your activities, show images and discuss events you have attended – it is a diary of sorts.

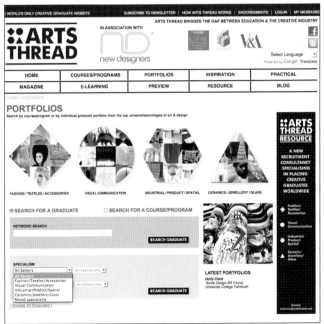

Above top: Kit Miles' website is simply but beautifully presented. You can find out about him as a designer, his collections and other projects, his press, events and contact details. He has organized his collections in named groups, showing a sample of designs from each.

Above: It is also possible to include your work on a site that promotes designers' portfolios, such as Arts Thread.

CVS AND COVERING LETTERS

Most undergraduate courses or university careers services will generally offer you opportunities to develop a CV. A CV is a very important document as it may be the only opportunity that you have to sell yourself to a company in order to get a placement or job opening. You should have a standard CV that you then might tweak and edit for specific opportunities that occur. Below are some golden rules for writing a CV.

♦ It should be legible – choose a clear and professional font.

♦ It should always be printed on good-quality cartridge paper.

♦ It should have no spelling or grammatical errors.

♦ It should be tailored to the company you are sending it to, showing that you understand its business by choosing appropriate imagery and describing how your talents and skills would suit its needs.

There is also some specific information that you should always include:

♦ Your name and address in full

♦ Email address (ensure this is one with a professional tone)

♦ A personal statement outlining your strengths and abilities, reflecting the type of career you might follow in that company

♦ A section about your educational experiences in chronological order, with most recent first and identifying grades achieved

♦ Your employment history, stating who you have worked for with a brief outline of your role and your responsibilities

♦ Any specific skills or abilities that you possess

♦ Interests and activities

♦ Details of your referees or a statement that references will be available upon request

Your CV should be no longer than one piece of A4 paper (front and back). If you are sending your CV by email then send it as a PDF file as this ensures it will print out correctly.

You may wish to include images of your work; these should be very well considered and printed at high quality. You can include some small thumbnails in the design for your CV, perhaps in a horizontal or vertical row on the front page, or alternatively you can attach an extra sheet with a collection of images or designs. Ensure that you do not overcrowd the page and that you think about the overall look of the page, including the colour balance and compositional factors.

A covering letter should use the same font, paper and printer as your CV. It should be addressed to an individual, if possible, and should never be longer than one page. The letter should state which job you are applying for, or certainly suggest the nature of your enquiry. Outlining the most relevant points of your study and work experiences is a way of introducing the details you wish to be noticed on your CV. If you are applying for a job in response to a job specification then draw attention to how and why you meet its requirements.

CV

Sarah Jones   15 High Street, Nottingham, NG0 5ZB, UK
                Sarah.jones@email.co.uk; 0115 000 0000

Personal Statement

A highly motivated printed textile design graduate with experience of designing for both interiors and fashion markets. Enthusiastic, committed and reliable with the ability to communicate, meet deadlines and work under pressure.

Education and Qualifications

2013   BA (Hons) Textile Design, University of Eastwich.
            Specializing in Printed Textile Design: hand-printing skills with a variety of dyes; CAD design skills -
            Adobe Photoshop and Illustrator; prediction and forecasting; market awareness.

2010   Foundation Course in Art and Design, Highfields College.

2009   International Baccalaureate.

Employment

2012   Intern: Design Studio, London.
            Assisting the design team to develop their collection for Première Vision; tasks included collating
            mood boards, mixing dyes, mounting and finishing designs.

2011   Intern: Interior Textile Manufacturer, New York. During this three-month placement I was involved
            at all levels of design and production, from research and developing design ideas and contributing
            to the design collection, to being involved in sales meetings and checking production and quality
            control.

2011   Placement: Designer Level Textiles, New York. Supporting the designer's small team in the
            completion of the production of its new collection, which was then launched at New York
            Design week.

Achievements and Awards

2012   Finalist in the regional Society of Dyers and Colourists competition.

2011   Awarded a three-month paid placement with an interior-textile manufacturer as the winner of its
            set 'live' project during the second year of my course.

Memberships

The Textile Society; Society of Dyers and Colourists

Interests and Activities

Travelling, reading, cycling.

Referees

Available on request.

Your address
[include postcode
and email address]

Date

Name and position of the addressee
Department
Address of company
[include postcode]

Dear Ms Smith

Re: Junior Designer

I wish to apply for the position of Junior Designer, which was advertised in [*identify where you saw the job advert*]. I am in my final year at the University of Eastwich studying Textile Design, specializing in printed textiles, and will complete the course in June.

[*In this paragraph bring to the addressee's attention any aspects of your skills or experiences that relate directly to the position that you are applying for.*]

My final project is a womenswear fashion collection for a market-driven project developed around the concept of 'time'. The collection uses drawing and photography to capture the passing of time and is being developed digitally, as well as through exploring print-room processes to further enhance the surfaces of the fabric.

I am able to attend an interview at a time that is convenient to you and I would be delighted to bring along my portfolio to show my design skills and my technical abilities. Please do not hesitate to contact me if you have any further questions.

I look forward to hearing from you in the near future.

Yours sincerely,

[*Your signature*]

Sarah Jones

POSTCARDS AND BUSINESS CARDS

Although traditional business cards remain a useful tool, postcards are often the preferred choice of students when graduating. Postcards provide an opportunity to include a larger image of your work, acting as an effective visual reminder of your design skills. In addition, because they are often picked up at exhibitions, they also give the receiver useful space to write reminder notes on the reverse. In developing a postcard or business card you should consider the following points.

Whether you choose to have a postcard or business card, you should always ensure:

◆ It is printed on good-quality card.

◆ It has your correct contact details on the back.

◆ It has a professional email and/or website address.

If you choose to use a postcard, ensure that:

◆ The image represents your work and what is being displayed in the particular exhibition.

◆ The work is professionally photographed.

If you decide to have a business card, it is worth using a professional company to design this, but remember that the design needs to represent your identity and emerging brand, so:

◆ Think carefully about colour and font style in relation to your design identity.

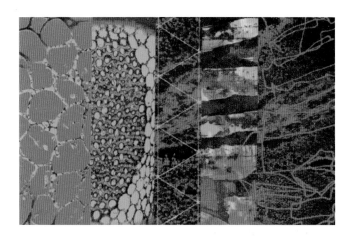

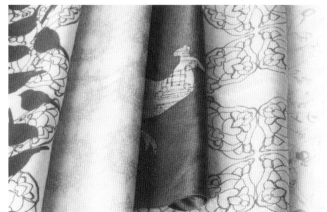

Designers in a professional context generally use business cards (left); however, graduates often use postcards (above) with an image that is large enough to show their design style and make an impression on the recipient. A postcard also gives those visiting degree shows the opportunity to make notes on the back regarding your work.

DESIGN COPYRIGHT

An important aspect of becoming a professional designer is gaining an understanding of design ethics as they relate to intellectual property (IP) and copyright. These issues have complex legal definitions that only IP lawyers can fully interpret. However, they are issues that all designers need to take seriously to ensure that they don't infringe on anyone else's IP or copyright. Equally, you should understand how to protect your own work.

Your intellectual property concerns the things that you create using your own personal vision, and can be the result of many types of creative endeavour, including design, music, literature, etc. In this context it is copyright law that relates to the production of textile designs or the drawings and visual research that you do for them. You own the copyright on everything in your portfolio. When someone wishes to purchase the work, however, then the protocol is that they generally also buy the copyright, which means they can use your design for as long as they like, on as many products as they like. They therefore need to be assured that your designs are your own work and original to you.

Until the point at which you have sold a design, try to ensure that you don't give anyone access to your work that might allow them to easily copy or recreate your designs; you need to be assured that your intellectual property is going to be treated appropriately with respect for your own copyright. In your portfolio make sure your designs are labelled with your name, a design number and name and, if you wish, a date and copyright symbol, for example: '© Amelia Rose 2010, design 00023, architectural flower repeat'. This asserts your rights and also demonstrates to anyone looking at the portfolio that you have an understanding of what those rights are.

Legal positions on copyright issues vary across international borders and therefore it is important to remain enthusiastic, yet cautious, if you are asked to send work to anyone either nationally or internationally. You should send work only to established and reputable companies whose ethical stance is assured. Sending low-resolution, small-scale images with a digital watermark would be one way in which you could consider sending a small collection of examples to show the range of your work. It is not advisable to send your whole portfolio or a full collection to anyone.

Your website might show some examples of the type of work you produce. Watermarking with 'copyright' and your name through the design is easy to do in Photoshop and signals your awareness of your rights.

There are organizations that you can join to help support your understanding of copyright and protect you further, giving you access to legal support if required. Anti Copying in Design (ACID) and the Chartered Society of Designers are two UK-based organizations, and at an international level there is the World Intellectual Property Organization (WIPO). You can also join these organizations as a student member.

SELLING DESIGNS

Pricing your designs should take into consideration the complexity of the design and whether it is intended for a fashion or an interior collection. While fashion prints may or may not be in repeat and are likely to be no bigger than A3, interior prints are always in repeat and may be 32, 52 or 64cm (12½, 20½ or 25in) in width; interior prints will generally sell for more.

You should expect to hand over your designs at the point of purchase, or arrange to deliver them at a later date. You should always ask the person purchasing the design for a business card with full contact details and it is essential that you ask him or her to sign a receipt before taking the designs away. Afterwards, you can send an invoice giving the full details of the agreed purchase, price and payment details. Some buyers, particularly if at a trade fair, may wish to pay by cash or credit card. It is also worth working out your design prices in a range of currencies.

If someone wanted to buy four or more designs, then providing some kind of discount would be reasonable and you should be open to negotiation. Your designs might be sold and presented with colourways and/or visualizations. If your designs have been produced by digital means then you should expect to hand over the digital files as well.

GRADUATING

Most degree courses offer graduating students an opportunity to exhibit their work in a degree show. This enables students to show a small collection from their portfolios in an exhibition-type context. The institution and the graduating cohort usually invite external visitors to view the exhibition at a 'private view', and this creates an opportunity for you to meet people from the industry to show your work, get feedback, network and hopefully sell work from your portfolio. It is important to capitalize on this opportunity by contacting anyone from whom you have had positive feedback.

Generally, your tutors will support your decisions about what to exhibit and show you how to display your work at its best. The show will probably have a unified feel to it across the whole course. Students may also be engaged with raising their own funds for their degree show; sometimes they may have to pay for premises, postcards, business cards and a catalogue. They may also have to pay for a graphic designer, photographer and stylists to develop their imagery and to help in organizing all the graphic elements.

This chapter has sought to summarize the skills and knowledge needed to practise as a printed textile designer and identify the final steps you will take to position yourself to embark on a rewarding career. While finding your first work experience or paid position may take perseverance, taking the time to develop your presentation, promote yourself professionally and follow up on your opportunities will deliver rewards. A career in printed textiles offers you a range of possibilities: to work at different market levels, to design or make products, to be expressive or follow trends and to create visually inspiring work with which people choose to decorate their homes or themselves. Few experiences will compare with the feeling of selling your first design, and most designers continue to enjoy that pleasure of seeing their products being sold and used by consumers – it is so exciting!

In addition to your degree show, there may also be opportunities to present your work in a national context: for example at Graduate Fashion Week or New Designers in the UK, where graduates from around the country exhibit their work. These events tend to attract more industry attendees than the degree shows, and often award prizes and offer other opportunities.

Above and right: Your college or university is likely to hold an annual degree show where you can exhibit your final design project. You should be able to invite people to come and view your work with the aim that you can make contacts, sell work or even be offered opportunities for work.

Right: You may also get opportunities to exhibit your work while studying by taking part in specific projects such as this one at the Rhode Island School of Design, USA. Textile and fashion students collaborated on a project inspired by archival material held within the school. These projects can offer you new learning experiences, material for your CV and images for your website.

GLOSSARY

Azo-free dyes – Dyes that are free of toxic, non-biodegradable, nitrogen-based compounds.

Bast fibres – Fibres collected from the skin, or 'bast', of certain plants, such as jute, hemp or flax (linen).

Bubble-up effect – Trendspotters look to the 'street' to help them identify new trends and cultural shifts as a way of forecasting new trends.

CAD – Computer-aided design.

Cellulosic fibres – Fibres derived from natural, plant-based sources.

Chinoiserie – Fabric with evidence of influences of Chinese style; these designs became common from the seventeenth century onwards.

Chintz – A printed, glazed, floral calico print. The style is mainly associated with India, from where chintz was imported to Europe in great quantities throughout the sixteenth and seventeenth centuries.

Colourway – One of a selection of colours or colour combinations in which a design is produced.

Colour wheel – A tool for showing the relationship between primary, secondary and tertiary colours.

Copper-plate printing – The process in which a design is 'engraved' or 'incised' to a flat piece of metal. Dye is then applied and the excess scraped away, leaving the remaining dye within the lines. The dye is then transferred to cloth using pressure.

Devoré – Chemical paste is used to 'burn out' the cellulosic fibres from mixed-fibre fabrics, leaving the synthetic or animal fibres intact.

Digital (inkjet) printing – Micro-droplets of dye, controlled digitally, are dropped onto fabric.

Discharge agent – A chemical that is able to remove or replace colour from a fabric that has been dyed or printed with dischargeable dye.

Disperse dyes – A dye type used for synthetic fibres.

Fast fashion – A term to describe the way in which trends and products alter rapidly, with several changes occurring throughout the traditional spring/summer, autumn/winter seasons. Criticism of this approach is that clothing becomes disposable and therefore uses excessive resources and ultimately contibutes to landfill.

Flash ager – A large machine that enables manufacturers to develop dyes and check colours very quickly; it steams, washes and dries fabric within five minutes.

Flax – This plant is the original source of linen fabric.

Flocking – A softly textured surface effect that can be applied to a fabric surface by printing a specialized glue and using heat to adhere the flock to the fabric.

Foil – A shiny, metallic or clear film that can be applied to a fabric surface by printing a specialized glue and using heat to adhere the foil to the fabric.

Gravure (photogravure) – A metal plate, or roller, is covered with a photo-sensitive emulsion that is exposed to a film positive, which is then etched. This can produce tonal and photographic effects.

Greige – Fabric bought directly from weaving or knitting mills in its raw state, prior to being dyed or printed upon.

Illuminating discharge – An agent that enables the removal and replacement of the ground colour with another.

Hand or handle – The term commonly used to describe the feel or drape of a fabric.

Illusionary prints – Designs that are printed to give the illusion that they are produced in another way: for example, prints that appear woven or knitted.

Indiennes – The identification of Indian design influences in a floral textile design.

Intaglio – This print method requires the 'engraving' or 'incising' of lines into a surface, usually metal, as in copper plate printing.

Intellectual property – Defines who created a design and therefore owns the rights associated with it.

Island designs – Where elements of the design sit independently from other elements, most commonly associated with copper plate printing.

Lyocell – A cellulosic regenerated fibre manufactured from renewable wood pulp, which is dissolved in an organic petro-chemical solvent.

Manutex – An agent used to thicken dyes to create a paste that can be pushed through the fine mesh of a screen.

Maul – A hammer used for applying pressure to a woodblock to transfer the ink directly onto the fabric.

Mind maps – Also known as 'brainstorming', the process of creating a mind map enables you to make free associations with your concept or theme as a way of identifying connections and ideas, and is an approach to starting your visual research.

Mood board – A board on which you can attach a range of inspiring images, words or colour chips that you have collected or found that are inspiring your project. It can be used to help keep you focused on the direction of your project.

Motif – Printed textile designs are often composed of one or more repeating elements, or 'motifs'.

Mulesing – A surgical procedure to remove skin, carried out on sheep to prevent infestation by insects. This process is condemned by animal rights activists.

Negative spaces – The space between the positive elements in a design; you may have too much or too little negative space. Negative spaces may inadvertently create an unconsidered or ungainly shape.

Ogee repeat – A lozenge-shaped image that is repeated using a vertical striped effect in either brick or half-drop.

Photo-stencil (positive) – A photographic stencil used in screen printing. Your original drawing must be translated into a format that enables you to create a 'positive'. This is then transferred onto a screen that has been coated with a light-sensitive emulsion by exposing it in a darkroom using a photochemical process.

Planned obsolescence – A method of moving trends on, so that consumers become dissatisfied with what they currently own or wear.

Prototype – Something that illustrates what a product or object would look like if manufactured.

Puff binder – A paste that can be mixed with dye and printed through a screen and which, when exposed to heat, expands to create a surface texture on top of the textile substrate.

Register – The degree of accuracy in the positioning of successive colours in an image. A design requires registering each time a colour is printed to ensure that each screen is positioned in exactly the same place.

Relief printing – A printing method in which the design is carved into the surface of a material such as cork, lino or wood. This is coated with the dyestuff, which is then applied directly to the fabric.

Repeat – The term used to describe the repetition of a design element or motif in the rendering of a complete design, ensuring that the design can be extended to print continuously across both the width and length of the fabric.

Resist printing – A method of creating images on fabric in which a 'resist' such as wax is used to ensure that areas of the fabric are protected from the dye that is applied. The resist can then be removed and applied to another area of the design to build up complex designs.

Resist – A dye-blocking agent made of wax, rice paste or clay.

Roller printing – A printing process invented in the eighteeenth century in which designs are engraved onto copper rollers so that textiles can be printed more efficiently.

Rotary screen printing – A variety of screen printing invented in the 1960s in which the screen is transformed into a rotating cylinder.

Sateen repeat – Sateen or spot repeat makes use of motifs placed on a rectangular grid to give a multidirectional or random appearance to a design.

Screen printing – The process of pushing a dye through a fine mesh. Also known as silkscreen printing.

Slow fashion – An antidote to fast fashion, whereby designers intend their products to be used over a longer period of time and/or consider their longer use and lifespan.

Squeegee – An implement with a rubber edge that is used for forcing dye through a fine mesh in screen printing.

FURTHER READING

Stencilling – The method of printing that uses positive and negative imagery to isolate areas that can be printed in one colour.

Strié – A subtle, tonal vertical-stripe effect often used in traditional wall coverings and textiles.

Substrate – A term used to describe a surface, such as fabric or paper.

Sustainability – A term used in association with the production and printing of textiles to evaluate whether these processes are considerate of their impact on the environment.

Swatch books – Books that show design samples, whether for students to show clients a range of designs, or for retailers to show interior collections alongside photographs with the fabrics and wallpapers in situ.

Tear sheets – Images or ideas from magazines or the Internet, often used as part of a mood board in order to help inspire your project.

Tjanting – A metal tool for drawing with hot wax directly onto fabric; used in resist printing.

Tjap – A mechanical tool for applying wax to fabric, used in resist printing.

Toile – A fabric prototype of a garment.

Toile de Jouy – A print style from the eighteenth century, most commonly associated with copper plate printing. The name toile de Jouy comes from the village of Jouy in France where this method of printing was perfected. Idealized village scenes with island repeats in one colour are very common in this type of print.

Tossed repeat – A repeating pattern that is designed to look random.

Tramlines – These appear when a design has been created in repeat but the connections between the repeating unit have not been fully integrated.

Transfer printing – The process of using heat to transfer imagery from one substrate to another, generally paper to fabric.

Trickle-down effect – Trendspotters look to a 'high' designer level to help them identify and forecast new trends.

Trompe l'œil – The use of hyper-real images to create an illusion of a three-dimensional object in two dimensions.

Upcycling – Using waste textiles, either pre- or post-consumer, and adding value to them by printing or stitching, making them into new products.

Voile – A woven, lightweight, semi-sheer fabric.

Woodblock printing – A design is engraved into wood, pressed into dye and then printed onto fabric. This type of method is known as a relief printing method.

CAREERS

Brown, C., *Fashion and Textiles: The Essential Careers Guide*, Laurence King, London, 2010

Goworek, H., *Careers in Fashion and Texiles*, Blackwell Publishing, Oxford, 2006

COLOUR

Anderson Feisner, E., *Colour*, Laurence King, London, 2006

DIGITAL TEXTILE DESIGN

Bowles, M. and Isaac, C., *Digital Textile Design*, Laurence King, London, 2009

Tallon, K., *Digital Fashion Print*, Batsford, 2011

FABRIC

Baugh, G., *The Fashion Designer's Textile Directory*, Thames and Hudson, London, 2011

Hallet, C. and Johnston A., *Fabric for Fashion*, Laurence King, London, 2010

FASHION

Fernandez, A., *Fashion Print Design*, A&C Black, London, 2010

Fogg, M., *Print in Fashion*, Batsford, London, 2006

INTERIORS

Fogg, M., *Couture Interiors*, Laurence King, London, 2008

NEW TECHNOLOGY

Lees, S., *Fashioning the Future*, Thames and Hudson, London, 2003

Seymour, S, *Fashionable Technology*, Springer Wien, New York, 2008

Quinn, B., *Textile Futures*, Berg, Oxford, 2010

PRINTING

Wells, K., *Fabric Dyeing and Printing*, Conran Octopus, London, 2000

SUSTAINABLE DESIGN

Black, S., *Eco-Chic: The Fashion Paradox*, Black Dog, London, 2011

Brown, S., *Eco-Fashion*, Laurence King, London, 2011

Fletcher, K., *Sustainable Fashion and Textiles: Design Journeys*, Routledge, London and New York, 2008

TEXTILE DESIGN

Clarke, S., *Textile Design*, Laurence King, London, 2011

Edwards, C., *How to Read Pattern: A Crash Course in Textile Design*, Herbert Press, 2009

Gale, C. and Kaur, J., *The Textile Book*, Berg, Oxford, 2002

Gale, C. and Kaur, J., *Fashion and Textiles*, Berg, Oxford, 2004

Quinn, B., *Textile Designers at the Cutting Edge*, Laurence King, 2009

Wisbrun, L., *The Complete Guide to Designing and Printing Fabric*, A&C Black, London, 2011

TEXTILE HERITAGE

Jackson, L., *Shirley Craven and Hull Traders Revolutionary Fabrics and Furniture 1957–1980*, Antique Collectors Club, Woodbridge, 2009

Jackson, L., *20th Century Pattern Design*, Princeton Architectural Press, New York, 2002

Mellor, S. and Elffers, J., *Textile Designs*, Thames and Hudson, 1991

Schoeser, M., *World Textiles*, Thames and Hudson, London, 2003

PHOTO CREDITS

pp.4–5 Emily Charman
p.6 Rachel Trenouth
pp.8–9 Sophie Bard of Love Bard Art
p.11 Anna Piper
pp.12–13 Sophie Bard of Love Bard Art
p.15 Courtesy Nahim Akhtar
p.16 Wendy Braithwaite
p.17tl Austrian Museum of Applied Arts/Contemporary Art, Vienna/Photograph: © MAK/Georg Mayer
p.17tr William Morris/Victoria & Albert Museum
p.17b Doreen Dyall/Victoria & Albert Museum
p.18tl Josef Frank/Svenskt Tenn, Stockholm
p.18tr Allan Thomas/Courtesy Liberty, London
p.18bl Barbara Brown/Victoria & Albert Museum
p.18br Scala, Florence
p.19tl Shirley Craven/Victoria & Albert Museum
p.19tr Alamy
p.19bl Barron and Larcher/Victoria & Albert Museum
p.19br Eszther Haraszty/Courtesy of Knoll Textiles
p.20tl Alec Walker/Crysede/Victoria & Albert Museum
p.20tr Jane Sandy/Heal's/Victoria & Albert Museum
p.20bl Anna White/Braintree District Museum Trust, Ltd, Warner Textile Archive
p.20br Emily Charman
p.21t Eddie Squires/Braintree District Museum Trust, Ltd, Warner Textile Archive
p.21bl Getty Images/AFP
p.21br Corbis/© WWD/Condé Nast
p.22 Victoria & Albert Museum
p.23t © Anokhi Archives/Photo: David Dunning
p.23c © Anokhi Archives/Photo: Suki Skidmore
p.23b Joyce Clissold/© Museum and Study Collection, Central Saint Martins College of Arts and Design
p.24tr Musée de la Toile de Jouy/Marc Walter
p.24trc Musée de la Toile de Jouy/François Goalec
p.24bl Timorous Beasties www.timorousbeasties.com
p.24bc Catwalking.com
b.24br Courtesy Jeremy Scott
p.25l Musée de la Toile de Jouy/Marc Walter
p.25r Victoria & Albert Museum
p.26t Bridgeman Art Library/Private Collection/The Stapleton Collection/© Estate of Duncan Grant. All rights reserved, DACS 2012
p.26c and p.26br Victoria & Albert Museum
p.26bl Tableau by Scheltens & Abbenes for Droog
p.27t Becky Early/Victoria & Albert Museum
p.27b Courtesy of Puma
p.28t Alamy/© fotoviva
p.28c BLESS
p.28b Getty Images/WireImage
p.29t Timorous Beasties www.timorousbeasties.com
p.29c + b Paul Smith
p.30t IKEA, designer Lotta Kühlhorn
pp.30b + 31t Courtesy of Ted Baker
p.31b Courtesy of ASDA
p.32 Mudpie Design Ltd/Fiona Jenvey
p.34 © Première Vision SA/Laurent Julliand, Stéphane Kossmann
p.35t *Amelia's Magazine*/Kingsnorth: Art direction Amelia Gregory, Photography Julia Kennedy, Styling Susie Lloyd, Illustration Laura Quick
p.35c *Amelia's Magazine*/Front cover: Art direction Amelia Gregory, Artwork Bruno 9li
p.35b Print & Pattern Blog by Bowie Style
pp.36–7 Louise Coleman
p.38 © Paul Willoughby
p39tl Joanne Bedell
p.39tr Wendy Braithwaite
p.39b Phoebe Moss
p.40t Zephyr Liddell
p.40b © Emma J. Shipley, 2011
p.41t Rachel Victoria Lillywhite

p.41b Amanda Briggs-Goode
p.42t Francesca Caputo
p.42c Elissa Bleakley
p.42b Sarah Patterson
p.43t Bethany Holmes
p.43cl Holly Betton
p.43cr Joanne Bedell
p.42bl Rachel Harris
p.43br Alex MacNaughton
p.44t Lucinda Dann
p.44bl Joanne Bedell
p.44br Bethany Holmes
p.45tr Nahim Akhtar
p.45tl Joanne Bedell
p.45c Phoebe Moss
p.45bl Emma Wolf
p.45br Jessica Beavis
p.47t Paula Love
p.47b Jessica Beavis
p.48 Courtesy Marimekko
p.49 Liberty London
p.51tl Fornasetti
p.51tr Erdem
p.51bl Getty Images/Gamma-Rapho
p.51br Image courtesy of Alexander McQueen/Photo: Bernhard Deckert
p.52l Designed by Angie Lewin for St. Jude's Fabrics. www.stjudes.co.uk
p.52r Courtesy Marimekko
p.53t + r Xiao Wang
p.53l Jessica Beavis
p.54 Sophie Bard of Love Bard Art
p.55 Design: Imogen Heath. www.imogenheath.com
pp.56–9 Victoria Robinson
p.60tr + tl Aimee Wilder
p.60l + cr Orla Kiely
p.60br Jane Gordon Clark for Ornamenta
pp.61–9 Sophie Bard of Love Bard Art
pp.70–1 © Michael Angove, 2008
p.72 Nigel Atkinson
p.73 and p.74tr + cl Sophie Bard of Love Bard Art
p.74cr Rachel Victoria Lillywhite
p.74b Nectaria Theodorou
p.75 Rosie Moss
p.76tl Jen Stark
p.76 tr Lizzie Allen
p.76c Neasden Control Centre
p.76b Tilleke Schwarz
p.77t Committee
p.77b Jane Gordon Clark for Ornamenta
p.78 Amanda Briggs-Goode
p.79t Rachel Trenouth
p.79r + b Amanda Briggs-Goode
pp.80–1 Dawn Dupree
pp.82–5 Katy Aston. Photos: Charlotte Hickmott
p.86t Romo Fabrics and Wallcoverings
p.86c Courtesy of Sanderson
p.86b Sophie Bard of Love Bard Art
p.87 Victoria Robinson
pp.88–9 Rachel Trenouth
p.90 Rosie Moss
p.91t Photo: Charlotte Hickmott
p.91b Shelly Goldsmith/Photos: Andra Nelki & Shelly Goldsmith
p.92 Alice Preston 2012. All rights reserved
p.93 Katy Aston 2012. All rights reserved. Photos: Charlotte Hickmott
p.94 Alice Preston 2012. All rights reserved
p.95 Katy Aston 2012. All rights reserved. Photos: Charlotte Hickmott
pp.96–7 Rachel Victoria Lillywhite. Photos: Charlotte Hickmott

p.98 Josh Goot/Shane Sakkeus
p.99r Paula Love
pp.99tl + bl Paula Love. Photos: Charlotte Hickmott
p.100 www.joannawilliamsdesign.co.uk
p.101 Sarah Patterson. Photos: Charlotte Hickmott
pp.102–3 Katy Aston. Photos: Charlotte Hickmott
p.104t Emma Molony
p.104c + b Martina Paukova
p.105 Katy Aston. Photos: Charlotte Hickmott
p.106 Suzanne Goodwin
p.107t Helen David for English Eccentrics © 1993
p.107c Georgie Worker
p.107b Dawn Dupree
p.108 Natalie Dawson
p.109t © NCD LLP 2008
p.109bl Orla Kiely
p.109br Corbis/© WWD/Condé Nast
p.110t Lucienne Day/Victoria & Albert Museum
p.110bl Helen Stevens, Surfacephilia
p.110bc Corbis/Historical Picture Archive
p.110br Centre for Advanced Textiles, Glasgow School of Art/By kind permission of the Estate of Lucienne Day
p.111tl Johanna Basford, 2005
p.111tr + bl De Joode/Soonsalon
p.111br Getty Images/WireImage
p.112t + c Hilary Carlisle
p.112b Devabrata Paramanik
p.113 Holly Fulton
p.114 Katherine Townsend/Photo: Catherine Northall
p.115t © Mary Crisp & Volkswagen AG, 2010
p.115b Sarah Patterson
p.116t Whaleys (Bradford) Ltd
p.116b Emma Cook, 2011/Photo: Neil Emery
p.117tr + r © 009 Textiles/Photo: Nicolas Dawkes
p.117bl Draw in Light
pp.118–19 Stone and Spear & Lucy Jay
p.120 Photo courtesy of Colorfield
p.121 Standfast & Barracks
p.122 Corbis/Maximilian Stock Ltd/Science Faction
p.123 © Myka Baum
p.124t + tc Corbis/AgStock Images
p.124bc Alamy/© Yang Yu
p.124bl Designed by Angie Lewin for St. Jude's Fabrics. www.stjudes.co.uk
p.124br and p.125tr + cr © Myka Baum
p.125br Whaleys (Bradford) Ltd
p.125l Liberty, London
p.126tr © Myka Baum
p.126cr Corbis/Kevin R. Morris
p.126br Whaleys (Bradford) Ltd
p.126l Corbis/© WWD/Condé Nast
p.127tr Corbis/Jacqui Hurst
p.127cr + br © Myka Baum
p.127l Louise Body
p.128t Science Photo Library/Eye of Science
p.128tc + bc GB Network Srl
p.128b Maxjenny/Photo: Lars G Svensson
p.129 Courtesy of Puma
p.130 Draw in Light
p.131t Science & Society Picture Library/ © Florilegius/All rights reserved
p.131b and p.132 Science & Society Picture Library/ © Science Museum/All rights reserved
p.133 Clarissa Hulse. www.clarissahulse.com
p.134 Science Photo Library/Philippe Psaila
p.136 © Dodie Sorrell
p.137 Corbis/© Michael Rosenfeld/Science Faction
pp.138–40 Standfast & Barracks
p.141 Insley and Nash
p.142t Standfast & Barracks
p.142b Paula Love. Photo: Charlotte Hickmott

ACKNOWLEDGMENTS

p.143t first2print
p.143b Swimwear by Graffinis Swimwear/Photo:
   Dan Forbes/Model: Jennifer Stano
p.144 Paul Smith
p.145t Bird Textiles/Designed by Rachel Bending
p.145b Designed by Louise Naunton Morgan, produced
   and sold by I Dress Myself/Photo: Louise Goodwin
p.146 Holly McQuillan/Photo: Thomas McQuillan
p.147 Ada Zanditon/Photo: Sarah Brimley
p.147 www.ethicalfashionforum.com
p.148 Tamasyn Gambell
p.149 Kate Goldsworthy, 2009
pp.150–1 Vallila/Designer: Tanja Orsjoki
p.152 Sian Zeng/Photo: Kangan Arora
p.153t © Celia Birtwell Ltd
p.153c Designed by Angie Lewin for St. Jude's
   Fabrics. www.stjudes.co.uk
p.153b Lucienne Day/Victoria & Albert Museum
p.154 Designs © Davinder Madaher
p.155t © Linda Thacker
p.155b © Linda Thacker for Zoffany
p.156t © Linda Thacker for Sanderson
p.156c + b © Linda Thacker
p.157 DEMANDINGMASS textile design studio, Spain
p.158 Taylor McArdle
pp.159–60 Photos courtesy of Colorfield
p.161 Anna Nelson/S&P Casuals Ltd
p.162 Emma Molony www.emmamolony.com
pp.163–4 Timorous Beasties www.timorousbeasties.com
pp.165–6 Side Five Designers www.side5designers.com
p.167 Prestigious Textiles Ltd
p.169 Lucy Wilhelm/© Friulprint SRL, Italia, ©2009
p.170 ©2012, Angel Textiles, Inc., New York
p.171 Designer: Freshwater Textiles www.
   freshwatertextiles.co.uk/Retailer: Feather and
   Black www.featherandblack.co.uk
p.172 Anna Nelson/S&P Casuals Ltd
p.173 Courtesy Anna Proctor
p.174 Image supplied © Skopos Design Limited
p.175 © Stephanie Jebbitt (Designs), 2000
p.176 Lily Rice/Photo: Kesara Ratnavibhushana
p.177t Mary Crisp/© Heal's 2010
p.177c © Mary Crisp 2010
p.177b Mary Crisp/© Victoria & Albert Museum 2010
p.178 Marian Lynch, The Colourhouse
p.179t + c Teresa Cole. Photo: Amanda Briggs-Goode
p.179b Teresa Cole. Photo: Charlotte Hickmott
p.180 Teresa Cole/Photos: Alan Duncan
pp.181–2 Dawn Dupree. Photos: Amanda Briggs-Goode
p.183 Lisa Anne Wilkinson/Photo: Colin Ross
pp.184–5 Kit Miles
p.186 Sarah Patterson: Printed Textile Graduate
p.187 Georgie Worker
p.188t Joanne Bedell
p.188c Louise Grant
p.188b Jodie Harfield
pp.189–90 Katy Aston
p.192 Beth Holmes
p.193tl Sophie Mazuryk
p.193b + tr Rachel Victoria Lillywhite
p.195t Kit Miles
p.195b Courtesy of Artsthread.com
p.200 Courtesy New Designers newdesigners.com
p.201tl + tr Roisin Kirby – Photo courtesy of
   Nottingham Trent University
p.201b RISD Apparel/Textile Print Collaboration/Hanna
   Soukup AP'13/Anna Ewing TX'12. MaryAnn Yi
   AP'13/Soyen Choo TX'12/Colin McGregor RISD/
   Brown Dual Degree'14/Kaitlyn Wheatley-Kitchline
   TX'12/Jenny Li AP'13/Jung Stephanie Song TX'12/
   Madeline Hinchion AP'13/Malika Dalad TX'12.
   Maria Canada AP'13/Laura Rider-Hill TX'12

Special thanks are due to: Laurence King Publishing, especially Helen Rochester, Anne Townley and John Jervis as well as Claire Gouldstone and Debra Johnston-Cobb for their continued positivity, enthusiasm and hard work to ensure the completion of the project. My colleagues at the Nottingham Trent University for their encouragement and support, in particular Julie Pinches, Nicola Francis, Pip Spoerry, Cathy Challender, Sue Pike and Tom Fisher. The Textile Design course team for their tolerance. The Nottingham Trent University BA Textile Design graduates who have supported the project with images, modeling and assistance with the technical elements of the book, in particular Sophie Bard, Georgie Worker, Katy Aston, Rachel Lillywhite and Sarah Patterson. Some time ago Anna Proctor planted the seed that there was a 'book' to be written and I would also like to thank her for her support.

I am most grateful to: Those who have been generous with their time and with access to their studios, workshops and businesses, in particular Linda Thacker, Ana Santonja, Colorfield Design Studio, Anna Nelson, Timorous Beastles, Side Five, Molly Freshwater, Mary Crisp, Teresa Cole, Dawn Dupree, Katy Aston, Standfast & Barracks, Insley and Nash, first2print, Stephanie Jebbitt and Charlotte Hickmott.

I couldn't have done without: The patience and generosity of Mark Goode, Max and Amelia Briggs-Goode and Ms Edana Gerrard-Morgan, who inspired my interest in drawing, pattern and all things textiles.

I would like to thank the following companies and individuals for responding generously: Rachel Trenouth, Anna Piper, Nahim Akhtar, Wendy Braithwaite, Emily Charman, Louise Coleman, Alice Hargreaves, Alice Preston, Mary Katrantzou, Tao, Anokhi, Musée de la Toile de Jouy, Victoria & Albert Museum, Vivienne Westwood, Jeremy Scott, Becky Early, Hussain Chalayan, Puma, Basso & Brooke, Paul Smith, Ikea, Ted Baker, Asda, Mudpie, Amelia Gregory, Paul Willoughby, Jo Bedell, Phoebe Moss, Zephyr Liddell, Emma Shipley, Francesca Caputo, Elissa Bleakley, Beth Holmes, Holly Betton, Rachel Harris, Alex MacNaughton, Lucinda Dann, Emma Wolf, Jessica Beavis, Paula Love, Marimekko, Cole and Son, Erdem, Holly Fulton, Alexander McQueen, Angie Lewin, St Jude's, Xiao Wang, Victoria Robinson, Aimee Wilder, Orla Keily, Jane Gordon Clark, Michael Angove, Nigel Atkinson, Rosie Moss, Lizzie Allen, Jen Stark, Tilleke Schwartz, Neasden Control Centre, Committee, Sanderson, Romo, Shelley Goldsmith, Josh Goot, Jo Williams, Suzanne Goodwin, English Eccentrics, Natalie Dawson, Nisha Crossland, Miu Miu, Surfacephilia, Johanna Basford, Rachel de Joode, Hilary Carlisle, Devbrata Paramanik, Katherine Townsend, Mary Crisp, Catherine Northall, Whaleys, Emma Cook, 009 Textiles, Draw in Light, Liberty Art Fabrics, Helmut Lang, Louise Body, Maxjenny Forslund, Clarissa Hulse, Dodie Sorrell, Bird, I Dress Myself, Holly McQuillan, Ethical Fashion Forum, Fashioning an Ethical Industry, Tamasyn Gambell, Kate Goldsworthy, Martina Paukova, Sian Zeng, Celia Birtwell, Emma Moloney, Prestige Textiles, SPC Casuals, Lily Rice, Marian Lynch, Lisa Anne Wilkinson, Kit Miles, Jodie Hartfield, Nicola Taylor, Ada Zanditon, Davinder Madaher, Taylor McArdle, Lucy Wilhelm, Angel Textiles, Gilly Thorne, Anna Scott, Imogen Heath, Simon Cook, Skopos, Louise Grant, Artsthread, New Designers, Nottingham Trent University and Rhode Island School of Design.